MOTHERLAND

Amanda Norman

MOTHERLAND

The Lived Experiences of
New Mothers Attending
Community Groups in
Developing a Sense of Self
and Belonging

The Gender Studies Collection

Collection Editor
Dr Jan Etienne

LPP

This book is dedicated to Xavier, Pandora, Cassius, and Lola who have taken me on an unimaginable life journey shared with others.

First published in 2024 by Lived Places Publishing

All rights reserved. No part of this publication may be reproduced, stored in a retrieval system, or transmitted in any form or by any means, electronic, mechanical, photocopying, recording or otherwise, without prior permission in writing from the publisher.

The authors and editors have made every effort to ensure the accuracy of information contained in this publication, but assume no responsibility for any errors, inaccuracies, inconsistencies or omissions. Likewise, every effort has been made to contact copyright holders. If any copyright material has been reproduced unwittingly and without permission the Publisher will gladly receive information enabling them to rectify any error or omission in subsequent editions.

Copyright © 2024 Lived Places Publishing

British Library Cataloguing in Publication Data
A CIP record for this book is available from the British Library

ISBN: 9781915734891 (pbk)
ISBN: 9781915734914 (ePDF)
ISBN: 9781915734907 (ePUB)

The right of Amanda Norman to be identified as the Author of this work has been asserted by them in accordance with the Copyright, Design and Patents Act 1988.

Cover design by Fiachra McCarthy
Book design by Rachel Trolove of Twin Trail Design
Typeset by Newgen Publishing UK

Lived Places Publishing
Long Island
New York 11789

www.livedplacespublishing.com

Abstract

In understanding maternal care beyond the home, this book invites the reader to explore how community groups, from co-operatives to virtual and charitable groups, have shaped and supported the social identity of their members.

It introduces topics about the value of preconception care and listening to new mothers during their lived experiences about having an infant. The history of health and educational care in England grounds the subsequent chapters in their explorations of the professional, as well as community and charitable support offered to new mothers in their transition to parenthood. In the latter chapters, specific examples of community groups specifically for new mothers are included as illustrative examples of the power of the collective's group and social identity in shaping, not only mothers themselves, but also their relationships with each other and their infants.

It contributes to the Early Childhood Education and Care (ECEC) dialogue about families and childhood from birth, with an emphasis on community care.

Key words

Community; belonging; connection; infants; care; relationships; parents; experiences in groups; therapeutic; love

About the author

Dr Amanda Norman is a Senior Lecturer (Childhood Studies) at the University of Winchester, UK. She is the author of *From Conception to Two: Development, Policy and Practice* (2019) and has published works about infant care pedagogies in academic peer reviewed journals and professional practice articles. She has also recently completed a book as sole author on *Historical Perspectives of Infant Care*, with Bloomsbury. Amanda is currently researching spiritual and infant care relationships, from historical and contemporary perspectives. As a trained practising therapeutic play specialist and early years consultant, she continues to support and liaise with early years professionals working in the sector, in addition to her academic role.

Author's message

The book is intended to be an informative guide about connection, understanding, and developing a sense of self in community spaces and places.. The book aims to be the catalyst in either developing your own community space and finding your tribe and reflecting on community spaces with new mothers.

This book aims to develop an understanding of how the collective helps shape a sense of identity for new mothers, as they navigate parenthood. It includes the nexus of past and present through examples to reflect on the power of social identity and the importance of community work in supporting parents and families. There is a specific focus on maternal care and the mother's experience, underpinned by attachment theory.

Note on language

In choosing the terms for the book, I have considered what I think to be the most appropriate and contemporary phrases often found in the literature or when communicating with groups, as well as in policy documents. I have also aligned terms such as community groups and mother circles that are familiar to those working in the UK.

Contents

Introduction

This book explores the lived experiences of new mothers attending community groups in developing a sense of self and belonging. The book initially considers the value of community groups and why a sense of belonging has the potential to shape and give agency to women's voices. In exploring this, I will be considering bell hooks (1999) and her thinking about sisterhood and solidarity among women, as well as her influence on thinking about love and relationships. Collective identity and feminist psychology will also underpin some of the conceptual understanding about the value of belonging as part of a community group. This initial chapter grounds the subsequent chapters on community groups, focusing on how new mothers have developed as a political, social, emotional, and spiritual movement in the spaces where they come together. Case studies will be included as a way of illustrating lived experiences, and this will be from the author's research and professional as well as personal experiences of being part of different groups, both as a women and a parent.

By parenting four children and working as an academic, I have had the opportunity to connect my research and personal experiences and the sense of belonging within a new mothers' group, I aim to share this and connect with others. Of course, new mothers' groups do not aim to devalue the roles of partners and fathers in parenting. Rather the book aims to focus on the understudied area of women as mothers within community groups. The groups catering for parents and infants discussed and shared in the chapters are predominantly attended by women in their role as new mothers. Perhaps in the way parents navigate their experiences at a societal level in England, mothers tend to predominantly attend these groups, without or with their partner. It could be argued that this is inevitable, and although fathers have attended groups on their own with their infants, these tend to be women-dominated spaces, with some groups (women's circles) intentionally clarifying that this is the expectation. I also argue that bringing in fathers' perspectives would widen the discourse and include paradigms about parenting beyond the scope of the chapters and indeed the book. I do however want to emphasise that the father's role is not subordinate to or less significant than the mother's role, especially in today's blended families. Throughout the chapters, I have referred to mothers' groups and parents attending groups because I want to highlight that some of the groups discussed are not exclusive to mothers. When I refer to mothers' groups, this intentionally includes women-only groups as well as attendance only involving women. To remain inclusive, I have also included those identifying as women and mothers when I share examples and acknowledge that I am discussing predominantly women's groups. I have decided to illuminate those identifying as women in their transitioned role as mother because I wanted to share how a sense of connection is created within the various agendas of the groups formed. I have begun with a historical lens on the power of the women's groups and aimed to include examples, perhaps less visible in the mainstream, although no less valuable than the more familiar groups. I have also focused on groups that have been contextualised within England as lived examples, although the lived experiences and notions of the group could be considered to be parallel to some international experiences of groups. While I wouldn't go as far as to say they are universal, I do consider them to be spaces and places that are found within and beyond England. I begin by sharing a historical lens because I want to include how groups have been formed. Sometimes groups, while often a collective with shared goals, have also been formed by external influences with the objectives imposed and in discord with the members assigned to the group.

Each chapter introduces a lens on topics including personal identity, relationships, and the groups available to new mothers. Within each chapter, questions and practice links are also included to invite further reflections and discussions about specific topics and issues. The practice examples are interwoven with anecdotal contributions.

The overall intention of the book is to give the reader the opportunity to submerge themselves in the world of community life and the value and sense of belonging that can occur through the lived experiences of being connected in a community. The aim is therefore to create a more intimate and subjective understanding of community groups, enabling the reader to delve deeper into understanding lives and questioning present and future social identity and belonging. This book also aims to develop an understanding of how the collective helps shape a sense of identity for new mothers, as they navigate parenthood. It includes the nexus of past and present, through examples to reflect on the power of social identity and the importance of community work in supporting mothers. A specific focus is on maternal care and the mother's experience, which is also underpinned by attachment theory.

It therefore contributes to the ECEC dialogue about families and childhood from birth, with an emphasis on community care. In recent years, the regular care of infants and young children has been increasingly sought beyond the home. Many parents place their infants into formal daycare settings as they return to work or opt to share their childcare. Subsequently, many settings that traditionally would have cared for and educated children beyond two years have opened their doors and expanded group care, providing 'baby rooms' to enable them to include the care of infants under two within their settings. Therefore, I believe the book is a timely addition to understanding and valuing the autonomy and strength in actively being part of a group and community where there is the time and space for mothers to 'be' with their infant. The book aims to foster among mothers a sense of self and confidence with their infant, rather than the often-conceived thinking of experts that can dominate the early experiences for novice mothers in their vulnerability when caring for their new infant.

In contextualising mothers' groups, an initial broad perspective about how groups have been shaped in the past will be discussed. This will be from the twentieth century and the beginning of hearing women's voices outside mainstream discourses. This will be illustrated with the lived experiences in the case studies presented. Revealing and sharing these lived experiences emphasises the power of the collective voice in national and political change.

What we mean by belonging and creating communities will then be discussed with reference to theoretical concepts and conceptual understanding. This focus then moves swiftly to the recent past with an oral historical contribution on how mothers were impacted by the pandemic. It focuses on how the nation moved towards virtual landscapes as a way of retaining and connecting new mothers who were physically isolated. In returning to a new normal, a national shift in funding and a focus on groups offered to mothers to enhance a sense of belonging and connectivity are explored. As a facilitator of such groups, I will reflect on my own experiences as a mother, as well as reflecting on the mothers narratives shared about what the group means to them as they embark on baby massage classes. Many new mothers seeking something less commercialised than baby showers but still wanting to celebrate the impending birth and arrival of their baby have found alternative practices with a focus on their spiritual meanings. Women's circles within and beyond the western view of religious practices have culminated in many women seeking and offering mother's blessings and naming ceremonies rather than baptism. The author reflects on her experiences where the community of connection and individual choice are part of the ceremony. In building a mother circle, there is a connection to the earth and thanks to each other, a space to reveal and be accepted in the here and now. This seems an appropriate and timely closing discussion of the groups I will be covering in the chapters that follow.

1
A historical lens to explore the value of mothers' groups

In contextualising mothers' groups, a broad perspective on how groups have been shaped in the past will be provided. This will be from the twentieth century and concerned with women's voices outside the mainstream discourses of the time. It will be illustrated with examples of lived experiences. Revealing and sharing women's lived experiences emphasises the power of the collective voice in national and political change and how groups are shaped and re-formed against the landscape of societal values and beliefs. In making sense of the new mother experience and the value of groups, I want to provide background on how new mothers are perceived and enter into and resist groups in their changing circumstances, sometimes not from their own willingness or desires. However, I have deliberately aimed to reveal the complexities in modern history about new mothers, but also the power of perhaps historically lesser-known groups of women that highlights the shifting discourses that continue to re-shape how we make sense of our experience as new mothers and seek ways of belonging.

Value of community of groups for new mothers

Pregnancy and the post-natal period have often been defined as being key periods in terms of the opportunity that they provide to equalise the life chances of all children. The state of the mother can impact on her capacity for parenting, leading to long-term consequences for her infant.

Care, wellbeing, and support from conception and pregnancy are positive for the infant, as well as the mother, in relation to the capacity to bond with each other when the mother feels emotionally safe and cared for. The risks of vulnerability are reduced and therefore the post-natal negative emotional states associated with this are reduced. With social support available to the mother, the aim is for her to feel good, resilient, and better prepared for the road of motherhood ahead. This can occur from pregnancy with the biological release of oxytocin. When this occurs, the good feeling enhances the bonding experiences. It protects the mother against physical pain, and a successful birthing experience helps mothers to feel supported and cared for. However, for many mothers, a traumatic birth experience can occur and thus rather than oxytocin the release of the stress hormone cortisol can cause further problems with an overwhelming feeling of anxiety. If this continues, then a tense and ongoing struggle to bond during this sensitive time may occur.

While the relationship between parent and infant being affected by mental health can set the trajectory for a child's later life and development, by focusing and targeting support on the ante- and

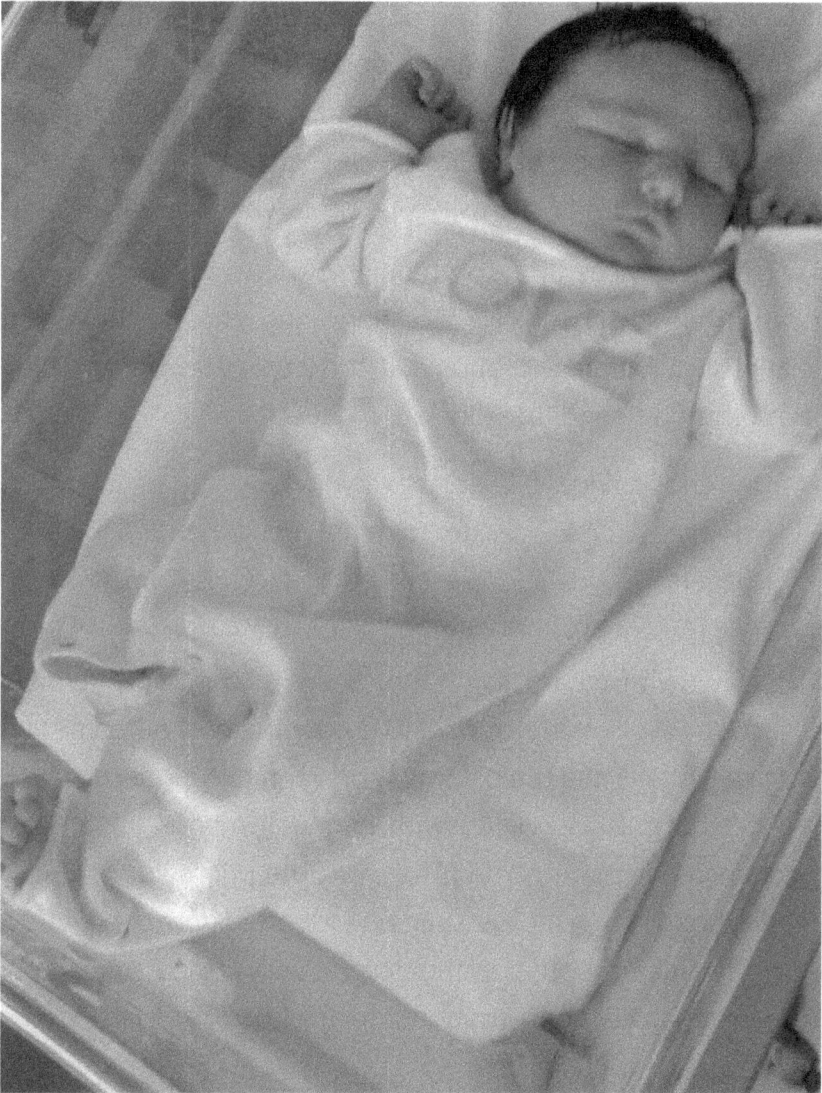

Figure 1 Love and connections

post-natal periods, there are still opportunities for transformation to occur. Drawing on the well evidenced studies around brain development, including the neuroplasticity of the brain, early intervention in supporting at-risk parents in a preventative model is an area where community groups can be helpful and support parents. The transition to parenthood offers both risk and hope for child development, and if families are supported holistically from the outset of pregnancy, greater impacts on the physical and mental health of infants' wellbeing can be achieved.

Therefore, services and community programmes and groups perform an essential role in supporting the mother-infant relationship. Different groups and services are available within the community, and these include:

- Universal services (aimed at everyone);
- Universal plus services (for targeted groups); and
- Partnership plus services (aimed at high-risk groups) with specific levels of intervention (Blair and Macauley, 2014).

The focus with regard to new mothers is to provide services that offer a preventative model to ensure the best outcomes for both the infants and the parents. A preventative model can help reduce the risks associated with maternal mental health and poor child health outcomes. Therefore, the priority during early motherhood is how mothers can be supported from conception, within the infant-mother relationship, as well as separately, rather than dealing with concerns about the child only at a later stage.

For many mothers, working outside the home is often romanticised by some feminist activists. However, in the twenty-first century, motherhood is no longer viewed as taking place primarily within the framework of a heterosexual marriage or even a heterosexual relationship. Today, families are constructed in many forms, including with parents of the same sex and with more than two adults sharing the parenting roles. While the focus of this book is on individuals identifying as women in their role as new mothers, there is no intention to undermine any others involved in parenting roles. Similarly, I have chosen to explore mothers' lived experiences because they align with my own lived experiences and my rationale that it is important to write about motherhood because it remains a relatively unexplored area in feminist theory (Pownal, 2021).

It should also be noted that considering new mothers and the community groups they are involved in is not about romanticising motherhood, by employing the same terminology that suggests women are inherently life-affirming and nurturing feminist activists. Taking this position reinforces the central tenets of patriarchy and male supremacist ideology, implying that a woman's fundamental vocation and purpose is to be a mother. This leads to the argument that if a woman chooses to not be a mother, focusing more exclusively on their career and creative work, they are somehow missing out and fated to live an unfulfilled, emotionally challenged life. Inadvertently it could be argued that not only should women, as mothers, assume the primary responsibility as the parent but in terms of living in relative poverty, they also need to ensure they are financially able to care for children as well, rather than decide not to have children. While women continue to assume sole responsibility for parenting, it is argued that society's propaganda undermines the complex and multi-layered roles mothers undertake. This is beyond the "stay at home or go to work" dichotomy often presented by groups, including women themselves, as a way of improving their circumstances. As bell hooks (1984) writes, female parenting is significant and valuable work which must be recognised as such by everyone in society including feminist activists. It should receive deserved recognition, praise, and celebration within feminism. Motherhood should neither be a compulsory experience for women nor an exploitative or oppressive one. Effective parenting should be done exclusively by women or in conjunction with men, and fatherhood should have the same meaning and significance as motherhood. Feminist theorists have also emphasised the need for men to share equally in child rearing but are reluctant to cease attaching special value to mothering. This illustrates feminists' willingness to glorify the physiological experience of motherhood as well as their unwillingness to concede that motherhood is an arena of social life in which women can exert power and control. While I have exclusively spoken about new mothers, it is not my intention to perpetuate existing discourses about motherhood, although I do feel that in contemporary society raising awareness of mothers' experiences needs more attention, ensuring both men and women appreciate the significant transition to motherhood. In England, new mothers receive up to nine months' maternity pay if they have been employed and up to a year of (unpaid) leave, in contrast to the government-mandated two-week allowance for the father. While I do not agree with this, it remains a reality and highlights the value society places on the roles of mothers and fathers in caring for their new infant. My justification therefore for writing about women is to focus on experiences in the new mother groups to raise awareness of the significance of community groups and thus signal the importance of this time for parents to be present in the experiences where they can.

According to bell hooks (1984), infants raised in black communities experience a different type of community-based childcare. For many black women living in poorer communities, there is often not the option to pay for external childcare as they must go out to work, so many rely on other people in their communities to help with childcare. Even in families where the mother remained at home, they would continue to rely on people in the community. This included everyday trips to the park and more freedom for the growing children because there was a sense of shared responsibility and trust in each other in the local community.

For hooks, it is also not about stigmatising parents but emphasising the need for collective parenting to help women, where parenting is delivered by the whole family and supported in the community. This is central to my own thinking about not just how the community is valuable but in what ways and how is it reflected on and experienced as a new mother. What is it about involving the collective group that is different to caring for an individual infant at home?

An example I will draw on to illustrate this further is a group that shifts from the personal to collective in recognising their positions as new mothers, their plight, the roles of their husbands, and that by being part of a group, they are able to influence the political landscape in which they live.

Social identity theory

Perhaps in an unexpected shift, but one that I argue is relevant to understanding groups, I have turned to Henri Tajfel's (1979) greatest contribution to psychology, his theory about social identity theory in understanding the psychology related to the importance of groups. For Tajfel, social identity is an individual's sense of who they are, based on their group memberships. He proposed that individuals come together for many reasons and that being part of a group is about gaining a sense of pride and self-esteem. Individuals coming together as a group therefore form a social identity and a sense of belonging to the social world. Tajfel considered what motivates individuals to come together and how they then view those who are not part of the group, the differences – or outgroup – and the similarities – the ingroup. An example of this is Twins Trust (UK) and how it has developed since its beginnings as an informal group (McLeod, 2023).

Twins Trust was initiated in a suburban front room in Surrey by Ajibha-Judi Linney, known as Judi, who had come to the UK from South Africa during the apartheid era. Judi was unable to attend university in South Africa (despite passing the entrance exams) because of her colour, so she responded to an advert to come to the UK where she trained to be a nurse and subsequently qualified as a midwife and health visitor. It was when she was seven months pregnant that she found out she was having twins. On the organisation's website, she gives an account of her own experiences as a new mother:

> My pregnancy was good and non-eventful until I got to seven and a half months. My feet were starting to swell up and I was very big, so I went into hospital for an x-ray.
>
> I had one of those hospital gowns on for the x-ray, you know the ones that show your behind! I couldn't even do it up as I was so big.
>
> After the x-ray (there were no routine scans back then), I remember hearing my husband's voice, then the doctor's voice who was telling Howard (and not me!)

that we were having twins and that one "did not look very good."

I shuffled out of the room with bits on show and just remember saying, in disbelief, "twins"? I think I was in shock. I started worrying about money and the fact that my family were no longer nearby to help.

Then I didn't want to get too excited because I was worried about the second smaller baby and think I tried to protect myself a bit.

There were a few sentences in the Bounty book about having twins. But there were no classes, no brochures, very little information on looking after twins. I felt quite alone.

My first baby Zareena, was born and weighted a healthy at 6lb 1oz and the second, Shareen, was delivered by forceps and weighed 4lb 11oz. Both were taken immediately into special care with no opportunity for me to hold them.

The twin girls were OK, but that I was very ill. My blood pressure had skyrocketed and I had a post-eclamptic fit. I was sedated for 2–3 days which was upsetting as didn't see the girls at all, and it was frightening for Howard.

(Twins Trust, 2023)

During this time, she recalled, there was no understanding or support for mothers having multiples.

I was wheeled in to see them after a few days, but there was no encouragement to touch or hold them … but that's just how it was.

> No one I came across had knowledge about caring for twins, which I suppose is when I felt something needed to be done.

For Judi, it was an isolating experience, and again she felt like an outsider trying to come to terms with her experiences as a new mother caring for more than one infant. She described the experience as particularly isolating once her husband went back to work and, with no social media, she aimed to go out into the community. Unable to find a group, she created one herself. She stated that:

> Everyone agreed there was not enough information about having twins. I started a plan, I tried to find out where there were Twins clubs, I did some research in libraries, and I wrote letters to various health professionals.

With a couple of other parents of twins, she held a meeting at the NCT headquarters in London (1978) and this was attended by representatives from about 12 existing twins clubs across the country. Today the charity is a flourishing national support network offering online and in-person groups locally and nationally (Twins Trust, 2023).

Tajfel's central hypothesis on social identity theory is that members of an ingroup will seek to compare aspects of an outgroup, thus enhancing their self-image within the ingroup. While this may be applicable to groups such as football teams and cultural, political, class, and religious groups, I wonder if the same could be applied to new mothers' groups. As I progress through the lived experience of new mothers' groups, I am consciously aware that these groups may not work for all women and that in some groups there may be members who feel disconnected and not part of the shared social identity. I do not want to assume that by including many examples of groups that there is an assumption these groups come together and automatically connect because of the common factor of them each having a new baby (Tajfel et al., 1979). In considering Tajfel's theory, I feel it is helpful to reflect on the processes through which groups are formed and what motivates some women, though not all, to be part of the group they form or join. Furthermore, what happens when the "outgroup" is forced to become a group in its own right but not in a way that is purposefully navigated or led by its members? What if the members do not want to be part of this group? How then do the members experience these feelings, forced into belonging to a group of women defined as new mothers, outside of the societal norms expected of new mothers?

Motherhood, as I am sure all of us agree, is often an intensive and lifelong relationship for women that can have a significant impact on their identity, and the transition culminates in women re-evaluating their autonomy, physical appearance, and work, as well as shifts in understandings about themselves and in relation to others. Women's self-reconstruction also faces the realities of motherhood in juxtaposition to their ideals of motherhood. This is also interesting when thinking about how we would like to parent and the reality of what we can do within the position we exist in. This may be linked to religious norms, poverty, time, and financial security. When women who are mothers do not fulfil their ideal, they often feel guilty or blame themselves for their shortcomings as mothers, even if it is not their own fault, further compounded by society's ideal view of what a mother is. Since 1918, groups for mothers, such as the National Council for the Unmarried Mother and her Child, have existed. In the aftermath of the First World War (1918), many women found themselves with a child and without a partner to help raise them. Single-parent families received little protection from government, and many faced a life of poverty. Responding to the needs of single parents, the organiser Lettice Fisher, a former social worker and economist, decided to act. She formed the National Council for the Unmarried Mother and her Child in February 1918. In 1930, unmarried mothers also became entitled to receive benefits from the government, as opposed to having to rely on charity or having to access what were previously the workhouses for the poor. However, the stigma of being part of this group has been compared negatively to those who have married, as a married couple would have at least some financial self-sufficiency. Therefore, those who fall outside of what society categorises as being part of new motherhood are then impacted by other women in the communities in which they live, and the beliefs and attitudes of others, as well as themselves, in the circumstances in which they transition to motherhood (Norman, 2022).

Being part of an outgroup in society: The lasting impact on women as new mothers

In England, the cultural context of the mid- to late twentieth century was a relatively stable uniformity of life, evolved around visible rites of passage, a cycle of school, marriage, work, and retirement. These predominant life aims were generational patterns and provided a moral compass to guide individuals, often complemented by a religious framework for life, in navigating a purpose to their rites of passages. However, as the political and economic climate has shifted, alongside the accelerated use of technology, rites of passage, including marriage and employment, have been met with growing uncertainty and challenge. Employment has become less predictable, and with more consumer freedom and geographical movement, family life has mirrored the change. As one of the oldest and most significant social institutions around the world, families continue to exist but as a social construct evolve and adapt to society's values as these change over time. Women's groups, comprising individuals of varying ages, have developed relationships and been conceived as purposeful ways to build strength, resilience, and moral values for the future support of new mothers.

However, it is also important to remember that some community groups were managed by charities and the state with a central rationale of promoting morality and attitudes that reflected the wider society's outlook about mothers and their babies (Seppälä et al., 2022). Membership of these groups could be enforced, with attendance being made mandatory even though the members might not agree with the objectives set by the organisers of the group. As Tajfel highlights about ingroups, what happens when women who are deemed to be on the margins of society become pregnant?

Every year from 1957 to 1961, London County Council placed approximately 1,000 women into designated mother and baby homes. It was not until the 1970s that a pervasive secrecy about unmarried motherhood, cohabitation, and similar "irregular" practices, especially among the middle classes, began to change to greater openness. According to Bloom (1995), teenage mothers were not regarded as distinct from older single mothers. Instead, women were divided according to whether it was their first or second pregnancy; those failing to "learn their lesson" were seen as corrupting. However, it was in the late 1950s that government officials argued that teenage mothers should be housed separately, to keep them away from repeat offenders and to enable the government to provide them with schooling and longer-term support. These outgroup members were shunned and encouraged to behave according to society's values, and motherhood out of wedlock was not deemed to be an acceptable aspect of this society. Another factor in the popularity and increase of mother and baby homes was the influential external drivers leading to changing attitudes about institutional care. During this time, institutional care came to be deemed inappropriate, and it was thought that foundling hospitals and workhouses, as well as group homes run by charities such as Barnardo's, had had their day and didn't align with current thinking about child development and child-rearing approaches. Furthermore, as illegitimacy rates rose to high levels in the mid-twentieth century, there was also a strong pull from childless parents wanting to create an aspirational family life and therefore seeking babies to adopt.

During the changing social climate of the 1960s, there was an increase in promiscuity and sexual activity that led to a further increase in fertility rates. Social changes saw a rise in the use of the contraceptive pill, as well as a steady increase in cohabitation. Despite the Abortion Act of 1967, there was still a high incidence of marriage in the younger age group who became pregnant and, in doing so, conformed to family values. Pat Thane's (2011) study concurred that the real cultural changes of the 1960s co-existed with strong continuities. The "illegitimacy" rate rose sharply over the decade, but attitudes changed more slowly.

Mother and baby homes as a hidden and silenced micro community

The primary purpose of the mother and baby homes of the twentieth century was therefore to provide unmarried girls with accommodation and support before, during, and after the birth of their illegitimate children. The secondary purpose was to give time during the period of support for decisions to be made about the future, the outcome of which could be to have a child adopted. The homes were widely distributed geographically so that a place distant from home where she would not be recognised could be found for any girl, such was the stigma against her. These mother and baby networks, sometimes themselves adoption agencies, provided a route for the mother to place a child.

Prejudice against a daughter and her illegitimate child and lack of family support for the future were perceived as the main reasons for girls going into homes to give birth. Here, the more usual view of family and community as supporting structures is reversed, with the rejection by the family of a young girl with an unborn child in the face of the prejudice of the community of which she was a part. Adoption therefore offered a fresh start for the mother and for the child who would have the security of two parents and be free of the illegitimacy label that they would otherwise have carried. Once in the homes, the girls found temporary support from others in similar situations, with the homes offering before and after care. The homes had dormitories for the women, communal living spaces, gardens, nurseries for the infants, and some included their own medical ward. Residents followed a daily schedule of chores, meals, prayers, caring for their babies, and recreational time, which frequently allowed for visitors and trips into town. The experiences of the women varied in the homes, just as the circumstances of their pregnancies varied; some found the homes more extreme while others discovered a welcome refuge. In the movement for an adoption apology, these mothers' voices have been documented as evidence about their circumstances. The membership of the group was at odds with the societal and political agendas about the families they lived in during this period.

Their voices on their life experiences as new mothers below illustrate how personal circumstances did not align with the community in which they lived. While only a few examples are shared, they reveal the tensions involved in belonging to this group.

> I became pregnant at age 18 in 1967. My parents were strict and I knew that my pregnancy would cause great upset and difficulties and was very scared. I closed my mind to the fact that I was pregnant and managed to hide the fact for seven months. It was then that one of my mother's friends realised and told her. The reaction from my parents was just as I expected; my father

slapped me and raged at me and it was made very clear that I wouldn't be able to stay at home and the baby would have to be adopted.

Naively, I thought my parents might change their minds and let me keep him, particularly when they visited and my mother picked my baby up. I stayed in hospital for about one week and it was a difficult experience.

My parents took me to the home on New Year's Day 1967. It was a large, cold, detached Edwardian house. The matron showed us round the rooms and the nursery, and I was shown to the room I would be sharing with three other pregnant girls. I think there were about 15–20 girls there aged from 14 to 25. We were expected to be there for six weeks before the birth and six weeks after. By this stage, I was quite relieved to be leaving home as the atmosphere had become very strained.

Although the regime was quite harsh, I felt relieved to be away from the atmosphere at home, and the camaraderie with the other girls there was good. We all supported each other, and although there were hard times when babies were taken for adoption, there were also some fun times.

(Movement for an Adoption Apology, 2023)

By the 1970s, the mother and baby homes had had their day. Adoption agencies closed or amalgamated, and their names no longer always reflected their religious affiliations. Social service departments were created in 1974, and local authorities became adoption agencies.

As discussed, in the mid- to late twentieth century, there remained a tremendous stigma, even from women who were married, about those who fell pregnant out of wedlock, and in particular those in their younger years – teenagers. Throughout history, they have been termed "fallen" women and viewed negatively by those in the ingroup of motherhood. In challenging these discourses, more informal groups have developed, and today some have grown into national charities, their beginnings being individuals wanting to use being part of an outgroup in forming their own ingroup, developed by themselves as a member rather than enforced by others (Matthews, 2005).

An example of this is a charity group known as Gingerbread (a charity for single parents), with its historical roots grounded in circumstances beyond the mother's control and often impacted by the cultural landscape in which they lived. While events beyond the personal are out of their control, views and perspectives about motherhood remain, regardless of circumstances. Gingerbread continues to support single-parent families today, and has done so since its first meeting organised in 1970 by Tessa Fothergill, a single mother living in London. She decided to start a support group for other parents like her to help combat some of the loneliness she felt. A new charity was therefore formed, and this provided support groups, titled Gingerbread, and named after the café where the first support group met. This highlights the value of both informal and more formalised groups offered in the community. Significantly, in 1987, after 69 years of campaigning, the Bastardy Acts were finally repealed. The Family Law Reform Act was introduced, which gave the same legal rights to children born outside of marriage as those born within marriage. For those children and families, this meant the stigmatisation of single-parent families was finally shifting, reducing their rejection as an outgroup and the comparison to new motherhood. In the twenty-first century, the charity has the strapline "single parents, equal families" and offers advice, practical support, and influential campaigning.

In thinking about the types of groups and what they offer to mothers, there is inevitably something beyond their infants that mothers have in common with each other. Tajfel considered that there is a pattern to this and identified specific areas to illustrate this further.

Categorisation

Categorisation involves shaping how we understand and identify with people. In this way, a new mother begins by seeking out what appeals to her and aligns with her thinking about new motherhood in terms of usefulness and connection to her identity before she became a mother. This could include seeking out **baby walking** groups for those who want to continue an outdoor activity they previously enjoyed. They may join a religious group or if they have twins, for example, join a twins group. In finding out things about ourselves and knowing what categories we belong to, we can define appropriate behaviour by reference to the norms of groups we belong to or would like to belong to.

Social identification

During the second stage, social identification, a group's identity is adopted and an individual categorises themselves as belonging to the group. This can be true for yoga groups where mothers think beyond the class to their practice at home, what they eat, what they drink, and the clothes they wear. All of these contribute to their identity as being a member of a group who regularly practises yoga. There will often be an emotional significance to the self-identification with a group, and self-esteem becomes bound up with group membership. You therefore pay particular attention to ingroup members and adopt their values, attitudes, appearance, and behaviour.

Social comparison

The final stage is known as social comparison. Once categorised as part of a group and identified with that group, we tend to compare that group with other known groups. If our self-esteem is to be maintained, our group needs to compare favourably with other groups, and I think this is particularly true for groups offered to new mothers. This can include baby massage classes and baby signing classes and how relevant and helpful we think these are, and therefore the motivation to attend these groups weekly. In the community, there is often more than one group offering the same service, and it is interesting to see how individuals compare other groups negatively with their own in maintaining the sense of self-esteem bound up with continuing to attend 'their' group. Competition and hostility can occur at many levels, and these can be motivated by financial reasons, numbers of attendees, and the type of service offered. Knowing this situation exists helps us to reflect on the strength of the group in itself rather than being concerned about any possibility that this could be reduced (Tajfel et al., 1979).

The distinction from personal identity is that social identity refers to people's self-categorisations in relation to their group memberships, whereas personal identity refers to the unique ways in which people define themselves as individuals. For example, this might include people's personal interests and values. By including the domains of both personal identity and social identity, self-categorisation has been developed. This considers that, dependent on the social context, more of the personal or social identity may be revealed. An example of this is that if we are alone or interacting with a close friend, our personal identity may guide our behaviour and thinking. However, when we interact within a group, our social identity may be more apparent. I have explored some historical mothers' groups to illustrate this further. I have considered how they have emerged and included personal identity in shaping the social identity of the group as a collective.

Moving towards the power of groups: A herstory and the impact of belonging

An abundance of research exists about motherhood and the processes of becoming a mother, and although some research has suggested that women change their personal identities in a variety of ways when they become mothers, there has been limited research about how women's identities, from their own lived experiences, have changed when they become mothers. What seems to be lacking therefore is literature about how women's identities change when they become mothers, based on women's personal experiences. I argue that theory can only capture one perspective on motherhood and the varied nuances of becoming a mother; what it means is a subjective experience. As I have introduced Tajfel, I recognise that this could be contested, and for many, identity is believed to have developed independently from others (Freud, 1966), while other theorists have claimed that identity is developed in the context of relationships and that women in particular tend to view themselves within the web of relationships they exist in, helping define who they are. As an example of this, I have included the voices of a group of working women to explore how, as a group, they were able to share a collective voice about their lived experiences as new mothers. In being able to record their voices through letter writing, I have argued that they have been able to gain a sense of self and develop a sense of self-awareness, proud of the group they belong to (McLeod, 2023).

During the late nineteenth century, working-class women in England continued to have little access to medical care, nutritious food, and domestic help. In a bid to support the women in Co-Operative Groups, the wives of the Co-Operative men formed what was known as the Women's Guild. As a group, the Women's Guild was a socialist consumer-based organisation designed to put the community in control. The Women's Guild's lead during this period was Margaret Llewelyn Davies. It was a group that provided an opportunity for women to become part of a movement alongside their husbands. As a small subgroup of the Co-Operative, the women met together. Buying items from the Co-Operative and being part of the organisation meant they not only benefited in terms of material goods but also by meeting regularly and sharing their stories together with other women. As the Women's Guild members grew in number, the organisation strengthened, becoming a platform for women's rights and community activism. One area of this was the issue surrounding maternity (Tilghman, 2003).

In forming a social identity, the lead of the Women's Guild, Margaret Llewelyn Davies, sought to gather testimonies on members' living conditions. In 1910, she asked them to submit evidence about matrimonial causes. She gathered opinions and personal experiences, and these were published in a book commonly known as *The Maternity Letters*.

The book led to the legal and medical professions communicating with the Women's Guild. *The Maternity Letters* targeted audiences both within and beyond the Co-Operative movement and at local and national levels. It exposed the private experiences of many women to the public, and because the experiences incorporated stories about social abuse, the impact of *The Maternity Letters* was to effectively raise public consciousness and motivate legislators. It also spread the virtues of the Co-Operative movement and gave recognition to them (Cohen, 2020). The reader gets a glimpse of women's lives, with records of 400 lives having been received by the Women's Guild. *The Maternity Letters* ultimately published 160 letters as representative of the 400 (Davies, 1978).

Replies were received from 386 Women's Guild members covering 400 cases, with a few from non-members. In analysing the letters, I have highlighted and themed women's reflections in the letters on being a mother and their experiences as part of the Women's Guild.

Husbands' role in conceiving

My husband's wages was very unsettled, never exceeded 30s., and was often below the sum. I earned a little all the time by sewing. Did all the housework, washing, baking, and made all our clothes. But no amount of State help can help the suffering of mothers until men are taught many things in regard to the right use of the organs of reproduction, and until he realises that the wife's body belongs to herself, and until the marriage relations takes a higher sense of morality and bare justice. And what I imply not only exists in the lower strata of society, but is just as prevalent in the higher. So it's men who need to be educated… suffering comes to the mother and child through the father's ignorance and interference. Pain of body and mind, which leaves its mark in many ways on the child.

(Davies, 1978, p. 13)

I am afraid I cannot tell you very much, because I worked too hard to think about how we lived. When my second baby came, I did not know how I was going to keep it. When the last one came, I had to do my own washing and baking before the week-end. Before three weeks I had to go out working, washing, and cleaning, and so lost my milk and began with the bottle. Twice I worked within two or three days of my confinement. I was a particularly strong woman when I married. There is not much strength left. But, thanks be to God, I have not lost one. I have two girls and three boys, every one strong and healthy.

The firm my husband worked for failed; then for the most times he did not work; but I can truly say that for the most part of twenty-five years 17s. per week was the most I received from him.

(Davies, 1978, p. 116)

Personal health

During pregnancy I always looked to my diet, and as my husband never got more than 24s. 6d. per week, I had not much to throw away on luxuries. I had plain food, such as oatmeal and bacon, and meat, plenty of bread and good butter… I never had a doctor all the time I was having children. I have had six, one dead.

During my labour I was never bad than for about three or four hours. I felt I could get out of bed the first day, and I never had the doctor, only an old midwife …

I must say that I am a staunch teetotaller, and have been all my life. I think that drink has a lot to do with some women's sufferings.

I had one child born without a midwife…

During part of the time we had a lodger, who paid us 11s., which helps us a bit … we were quite comfortably off.

(Davies, 1978, p. 10)

Cleanliness has made rapid strides since my confirnments; for never once can I remember having anything but face, neck, and hands washed until I could do things myself …

For a whole week we were obliged to lie on clothes stiff and stained, and the stench under the clothes was abominable, and added to this we were commanded to keep the babies under the clothes.

I often wonder how the poor little mites managed to live, and perhaps they never would have done but for our adoration, because this constant admiration for our treasures did give them whiffs of fresh air very often.

(Davies, 1978, p. 19)

Length of time during pregnancy

I was glad to get up and get about again before I was able, because I could not afford to pay a woman to look after me. I kept on like that till the sixth little one was expected, and then I had all the other little ones to see after. The oldest one was only ten years old, so you see they all wanted a mother's care. About two months before my confinement the two youngest fell ill with measles, so I was obliged to nurse them…

For twenty years I was nursing or expecting babies. No doubt there are others fixed the same way as I have been.

(Davies, 1978, p. 2)

The consequence was my third child was not born strong. She had a cough as soon as she was born. It was a struggle to put enough by to have a nurse in for a fortnight. I have had to get about to do my own housework long enough before I was fit to do it… My husband was working for Co-operative firms.

(Davies, 1978, p. 43)

In describing a sense of self, the mothers sought to contextualise their temporal personal identity within their domestic roles and lifestyles, life histories, and inter-relational experiences. Through articulating key formative events, the women sought to construct identity narratives that provided meaning to explain their personal circumstances. The social roles that the women identified were relational, vocational, and community-oriented. Relationships with others as well as responses (or lack of them) from others in these spheres contributed to how they viewed themselves. Over time, the women's self-awareness grew, and they became more insightful about their own strengths, values, and needs. This informed the resources and strategies they needed and accessed to support their mental health and wellbeing. Speaking out included addressing the issues around motherhood during troubling circumstances and times. The opportunity to share their stories, while their experiences were troubling, was empowering and cathartic for them. When the women began speaking out, they seemed to embrace their role as a core component of selfhood. Also significant were the women's impending opportunities and obstacles related to their ideas about their own competence, social status, agency, and aspirations. The findings also highlight that identity is inseparable from social connection, with participants describing the ways in which their sense of self was heavily shaped by interactions with others and in a community – a village. The publication of the women's life experiences circulated and therefore provided critical information about the ideological frames and normative constraints experienced by working-class women. This was specifically on the topic of reproduction and the economic disadvantages of infant care and support.

The letters described were a published testimony to their social identity and provide a deeper understanding about the value of being part of a group and having a sense of belonging. The women's individual voices in the published letters about their maternal experiences revealed their living conditions and how poverty and lack of understanding about childbirth had a lasting impact on their life. As a collective, they served the purpose of provoking a national response and a change in the law about access to and who receives the maternity benefit, which at the time went to the husband.

Against this landscape of macro groups and how historical groups – including state-run, voluntary, and charitable – have emerged in England, I will now explore the micro groups and what can be learnt from them in the twenty-first century.

Learning objective
Historical lens on community groups

To reflect and think about how community groups have been established historically and understood in the past, with considerations to their purpose and value for new mothers. Also consider the tensions with enforced groups and voluntary groups.

2

Creating communities that care

The value of listening to new mothers during their first year as a parent and creating opportunities for support

In delving deeper into belonging and creating communities that care during the first year of having an infant, I will discuss some more theoretical concepts and conceptual understandings and complexities of these groups in the twenty-first century. I have included personal reflections and the way we construct our interactions and how we can feel socially excluded from as well as included in community groups. In consideration of these areas, I have included what I consider to be valuable in creating positive, nurturing groups, for the new mothers with other mothers, but also as facilitators within the groups.

What is so special about early infancy and motherhood?

Prior to conception, parents may begin to visualise and appreciate their transitioning role towards being a parent. Winnicott (1953) described the infant as part of the primary carer, often the mother. Parents are not expected to become experts on day one of having children, and he argued that being a good enough parent would suffice in supporting healthy outcomes for their children. Good enough parenting was a defence against what Winnicott saw as the growing threat of intrusion by professional expertise that parents encountered with their infants. Winnicott focused on the nurturing environment provided by the parents for the infant. Infants create integrative and disruptive factors in family life, and in their emotionally healthy growth promote family units. The integrative factors from the infant's perspective include a degree of reliability and availability to which parents respond, in the capacity to identify with them (Winnicott, 1968). This is also determined in the way parents respond to them, and this transcends into their own potential capacities for parenting, strengthened and developed by the expectations of their infants. Therefore, in subtle and overt ways, infants produce a family around them alongside the parents' own knowledge about expectation and fulfilment as, in this case, the mother, although not precluding the father in their parenting role (Davies, 2014, p. 133). New mothers, therefore, are informed by their infants as much as they influence their infants. From the idea of it taking a village to raise a child and emotionally holding the parents within groups, we can proceed to consider how the community serves this purpose. However, by exploring and including the experiences of new mothers, I am also conscious not to stereotype groups or individuals as they navigate their new experience. I need to initially reflect on how I approach and consider my own position to be able to then evaluate and include narratives of other new mothers.

Being reflective has become a guiding concept in feminist research and how we reflect on our own position within the research endeavour of feminist research. For me, being reflective requires being able to situate my personal, political, intellectual, theoretical, and autobiographical self. During this process, I aim to develop and generate an interactional process of growing self-awareness in relation to the community group environments and from the perspective of others. This is from listening to the lived experiences of others or reading about their experiences. I need to think about the value of new mothers' groups and why they offer an important function in the private and communal lives of new mothers.

By researching these groups, I reflect, through a critical transformative lens and within feminist research, on how the groups can activate social change. By working collaboratively with groups and communities, I have noted how the groups are useful to a community and empowering for the women, through consciousness raising.

Critical transformation for me is about:

1. Being inquiry-based and open, grounded in people's lived experiences and concerns;
2. Being participatory as researchers and communities collaborate in the research process; and

3.   Evaluating the groups, and the groups themselves being transformative because they actively create change within the members (Pownal, 2021).

Carrying out research together, as part of a group, represents a shift from doing research on people to doing research with people. It also reflects a move which has been gathering momentum since the 1960s to ensure that academic research is of practical benefit to societies, communities, and organisations that have been embraced by feminist researchers.

This includes paying attention to how the power of those I am discussing influences my attitudes and behaviour, positioning myself as a woman, and mother, with others through a non-hierarchal relationship. I think I also need to be attentive to issues of voice and those speaking on behalf of others, especially mothers who may be accessing groups in the community. In narrating on behalf of others or representing the experiences and perspectives of others, I attempt to be inclusive. I don't want to inadvertently set out to colonise the stories and experiences of others without regard to their importance. However, I do recognise that by sharing my own experiences, I may be contributing to a colonial representation of how mothers "should" act and feel. I have therefore tentatively and emotionally reflected on this as I select the groups I want to share in a bid to ensure there are various voices and that, in reading them together, they are authentic voices and challenge their positions and representations in the communities in which they live (Leavy and Harris, 2018).

By actively listening to the women I have spoken to about their emotional labour as new parents and the work they do within and beyond the home as they seek to connect with others in the community, I have aimed to demonstrate empathy and support, applying my own feminist values regarding inclusivity and respect. In understanding this further, I have emphasised initially how I view myself not just as a researcher and writer but as a new mother in understanding and reflecting on the way I discuss groups I have engaged with and the others around me (Capdevila and Frith, 2022).

Personal construct theory, developed by Kelly (1955), evaluated the thought process of how we view ourselves. He proposed that every human constructs their realities (lived experiences) based on a hypothesis made about these situations. Individuals then test their hypothesis and refine it based on their mental constructs of their new realities. Mental constructs play an active role, interpreting knowledge experienced in the world through the lens of our constructs. These are also used to predict or anticipate events that determine our behaviours, feelings, and thoughts. All events have multiple interpretations and change according to how we construe relationships between group members (Kelly, 2013).

The relationships of constructs or concepts derive from the meanings they have placed on people's past experiences. Of course, we are all unique and therefore construe events differently and then base this on how we present behaviours in the present context we find ourselves in.

In thinking about this further, I have included a personal narrative of my mother's experience as a new mother and then mine as a new mother and how we both speak about our experiences. These extracts highlight the way we illustrate our entangled and yet also distinct experiences across two different timelines (Dallos, 2015).

A new mother's experiences during the 1960s in England:

> My children were born in the 1960s and 1970s and I have seen many changes. I think the support was much better in the 1960s and the 1970s. The health visitor was friendly but firm, and the doctor and health visitor were helpful with advice. I was told I had to do things in a certain way with my first child and this has stayed with me. I was worried I would get things wrong

Figure 2 Generational relationships

so I followed their advice. I would also be told off if I hadn't done what they said. I wasn't very old so glad to listen and do what was told of me. There were no mobile phones so I would have to go to the telephone box down the road with a sick baby for any advice if I needed it. My support network was attending regular clinics and having my baby weighed. I would also meet up with friends and we would go to the park together for a walk. This became a regular activity and we tended to do it each week. I found it was helpful to get out of the house and chat to each other although my main advice was from the clinic.

We have many different family dynamics now, so it is important to envelope both parents and siblings together and develop the family structure from this. I felt, when I was younger, I was not confident and felt I had to do what I was told. Now I would have more of a discussion, and I think this is important.

A new mother's experiences during the 2000s in England:

Prior to having my first child, I had worked full-time for many years and didn't anticipate being able to stay home for any length of time because financially it would have been too difficult. When my son was born, I regularly attended the clinics and would chat to the health visitor but would often question some advice. During the time, many babies wore amber beads around their necks as a teething prevention which I couldn't really understand and even my health visitor raised an eyebrow to the effectiveness of them. I attended baby sensory groups with my son and this was fun. We would go each week, and these were held at a local centre. I also went to nursery with my child after he was nine months as they had music sessions for babies during this time. I didn't feel very confident during the first few months but also felt quite critical and challenged by the differing advice offered. I felt I was doing OK but relied on groups and many of my friends had older children or none when my first son was born.

Both of us mentioned how we felt and the anxiety about being a new mother. I found it interesting that during this writing exercise, we both spoke about how we accessed support; my mother sought much more informal support and then advice from the professionals. I didn't get the impression she challenged the advice, whereas I felt I did. Maybe this was to do with our age when we became mothers – I was 38, whereas she was 18. I do think her approach to parenting must have informed me, and her reflections about not feeling confident were perhaps her trying to ensure I did not feel this way and felt I could question things if necessary. She also mentioned going out and meeting at the park. My experience involved accessing much more organised groups and being supported by both professionals and those offering activities for infants. It was less about "me" as a mother and more about stimulation for my son, whereas my mother talked about the park. Her son (my sibling) would have been too young to access the park as he was under one year of age so it was more about going for a walk and chatting to her peers in similar situations.

Personal construct theory and groups

In thinking about the value of new mothers' groups further, I feel there are useful aspects of personal construct theory to apply to community groups. This includes the capacity to observe and understand how mothers develop and change their constructs about themselves as mothers, as well as their understandings of their infants' behaviours, because of attending new parents' groups. The mothers in the groups I have attended would monitor their baby and construct their beliefs based on what their baby might be feeling, thinking, or needing and therefore respond to them appropriately. By attending groups, the mothers would obtain information and learn about new things, talking to other mothers and meeting new parents who were going through the same thing. They gain reassurance, and regular attendance provides a fixed opportunity and something to look forward to, making life a little easier and more enjoyable. Through new activities, mothers seek personalised information, support, and organisational services that facilitate their contact and interactions with other mothers (Bannister, 1977).

Groups can come to develop in many forms, from having expert information as the central aim to a simple opportunity to meet other mothers who live nearby, or as a way of combating the isolation experienced by new mothers. Such parenting groups facilitate information and advice and are important for outreach. They connect families and serve to enable early interventions in their communities as a way of sharing experiences.

Communities of new mothers' groups within the infant-parent dyad

As Tajfel concluded, people build their social identities from their group membership. They meet their basic psychological needs, satisfy their social identities, and therefore gain a sense of belonging in groups. The group members have a positive image and high status in comparison with other groups, and this leads individuals to attempt to maximise the differences between their groups and how they view other groups they don't belong to (Tajfel et al., 1979).

The social support of groups for many new mothers relates to their wanting to emotionally and physically feel that they belong. From this point of view, the group together can go even further and provide a protective function against depression for mothers. The members can promote mediation of self-sufficiency and a positive self-evaluation in parenting. The honest and trusting relationships, based on empathy, can be a source of support and form a strength-based approach in helping and supporting new mothers, recognising their strengths and abilities, with new challenges to their mental health and caring for their infant. I noted this in particular when I attended and facilitated infant massage groups. I discuss this in more detail in a later chapter but suffice to say here that the group members created bonds with their infants and each other during their six weeks of attending. Their relationships were also deepened by the discussions held. For many members, aspects of the process were carried through the gentle touch they shared with their infants, and this led the mothers to think about their own bodies in relation to their infants. They were able to authentically tune into themselves, and there were many conversations about how they "looked" prior to birth and now as a new mother. They talked about shape shifting in the embodiment sense, celebrated by some while others continued to feel insecure about their temporal body shape as they grappled with breastfeeding and physically tuning into their infant during the session. In recent years, some psychologists and other academics have turned their attention to the importance of embodiment because our bodies are central to our lives. This is an interesting aspect given that many, albeit not all, new mothers go through a physical as well as emotional transition and thus their identity is transformed. The way in which we use and manipulate our body shape to externally reflect who we are and our desire to externally project our bodies more broadly go beyond this discussion, but aligning our identity to our body is of course more complex than simply shifting the intake of food or increasing exercise. Time, motivation, and affordability can be managed but it must be recognised that changing the body is not always possible for everyone, for many reasons. For a new mother, the focus has predominantly shifted from her personal identity to her infant's and therefore the labour of feeding, caring, and good enough parenting may prolong the desired pre- pregnancy identity and physicality of the mother. In communal spaces that allow them to share thoughts and reflections on these issues, mothers can process and share their thoughts, and, as previously concluded, benefit from a strength-based approach within the group (www.mellowparenting.org/).

Of course, not all groups for mothers involve their infants always being present. Mellow Babies is a group programme specifically for parents of children under 15 months. The aim of the Mellow Babies group has emerged from evidence about the importance of the early months and the role of mother-infant interaction, as well as brain development. More recent evidence has also shown that good post-natal relationships can be beneficial in offsetting and buffering the damaging effects of stress that may have occurred during pregnancy and can result in post-natal depression or long-term anxiety and stress.

Mellow Babies group sessions last for 14 weeks and are generally attended by the parent for one full day each week. The programme addresses the lives of the parents using reflection and encourages them to share their own stories, and develop self-esteem and assertiveness. Cognitive behavioural interventions for low mood and anxiety are also included. During the morning, parents attend a personal group while the infants and young children are in a children's group. The children's group becomes a therapeutic group with carefully planned child activities drawing on the same themes as the parents' group (Leach, 2017).

During lunch time, the parents and children rejoin each other and share a meal, nursery rhymes, and songs. A joint activity is then carried out between the parent and the child as part of their close interaction process. The activities are also intended to be inexpensive so that the ideas can be continued and carried beyond the group. Some parents in the group may never have experienced certain aspects of play, and they can explore messy, fun play or craft activities. Visits to the local library or the park and local facilities are also encouraged. After the joint activity sessions, the parents go back to their own groups for a parenting workshop, and this is based around personalised video feedback about each person's interaction with their baby. An interactive activity such as feeding, nappy changing, or dressing is recorded at home by the parents, and this is used for personalised strength-based feedback on their video. When shared, this has improved parental sensitivity towards their infants and also developed their own reflective thinking about being a parent.

This is a particularly helpful group for mothers who may have been identified by the health visitor because of post-natal depression and scored highly on the post-natal depression scale.

An example of this was Nicola who suffered from post-natal depression. By attending the group, she was able to share and discuss the premature death of her disabled sibling during her own childhood and how this gave her somewhat morbid thoughts around mortality and young children. The interactions between her and her infant were warm and loving during play with close, mutually responsive interactions. However, caretaking activities such as feeding seemed to be an area of high anxiety for both the infant and the mother. During these times, Nicola presented as being tense and this was met by similar infant responses. Attending the group regularly began to build trust, and she came to acknowledge that her infant was OK if they were separated. By the end of the group's 14 weeks, she was recorded as being in a much healthier space (Leach, 2017, p. 199).

During my own experiences of being a facilitator of a group, I also supported parents whose children had medical conditions. The power of the group was immense compared to the work carried out on a one-to-one basis. As a community, the mothers were able to share their experiences, and while there were no conclusions or resolutions to some of the situations, the group provided a space for the parents to be able to be emotionally held. Similarly, we had separated times so there was space for the mothers to come together and chat during a refreshment break while the infants were being cared for in a different room. Some of the infants needed oxygen tanks and were medically poorly so being next door provided enough space for the parents to talk to other parents but be near if they were needed or had to be called for support by the staff looking after them. The latter part of the session then concluded with shared songs and stories using simple, handmade props that parents could make at home.

In further illustrations of the mental health benefits of community groups for new mothers, it is worth noting the charities that run new mothers' groups to acknowledge the benefits they provide. The Rockabye charity provides a small group that mothers (and fathers because they are not excluded) can attend to meet other parents, share their experiences, and spend time nourishing the bond between themselves and their infant. Attendees of the group agree that talking and listening to other parents can help them feel more confident and stronger as a new parent. Sharing the struggles that all new parents experience can help them feel that they are not trying to carry out their role as new mother on their own. The group is a non-judgemental and accepting space for you to share your difficulties. They include mothers who may have had a difficult birth experience or a difficult journey to becoming a parent. The group is a space where they can feel listened to and supported. Playing, singing, and doing activities are also part of the group, and these aim to encourage the connection between the mother and their baby. The programmes generally run for 10–12 weeks with a closed group so the same families attend for the whole programme. Each session is about an hour long, and there is a facilitated space for the parents to talk in a safe, non-judgemental, accepting atmosphere. The testimonies on their website include comments about the experiences the parents have gained from attending the programme. I have selected a few extracts to illustrate their experiences as part of the group:

> Brilliant! Made me feel at ease straight away, listened to me and made me feel like I'm not alone!
>
> It's been good to meet people, get out the house and be able to spend quality time with my baby.
>
> It's given me confidence to go out and be part of a group.
>
> Baby has become really sociable and he really enjoys the music!
>
> Lovely, supportive team.
>
> I've enjoyed Talk Time and listening to other mums' experiences. I've enjoyed the hour session to bond with my baby without distractions.

There are also comments about Antenatal Rockabye:

> Very, very helpful and very nurturing.
>
> Course leaders were fab, knowledgeable, kind, open and caring. It was well-structured while not feeling rushed. Loved it!
>
> Really helpful to hear and be heard.
>
> Lovely – a good opportunity to focus on the kind of messages you want to give your baby.

It was just the non-judgement of everything.

I just didn't feel a connection (with my baby) and Antenatal Rockabye helped me to feel connected, and I don't feel as worried.

(Rockabye, 2023)

The testimonies about the organised group facilitated by a leader highlight the value such groups provide to those who attend. Similarly, another charity, Mothers for Mothers, provides a regular group for new mothers. It offers maternal, mental health, and wellbeing support, advice, and information to women, birthing people, and their families. This charity is focused on mothers who have lived experience of depression, anxiety, and isolation during pregnancy or after birth. Their services include:

- Peer support groups;
- Peer support on the New Horizons Mother and Baby Unit (MBU);
- Art therapy and counselling (at the MBU and in the community);
- Antenatal groups;
- Peer support for mothers of children with special educational needs and disabilities (SEND); and
- Trips and events.

(Mothers for Mothers, 2023)

Figure 3 Crafting as a group

The tensions of community groups and the re-creation of groups

Of course, not all members of a group fall into place and collaborate harmoniously to reach positive outcomes. The charities described above may aim to achieve these positive outcomes, but for some mothers, the realities can be quite different. Rather than shying away from or ignoring the challenges of these groups, I feel it is worth considering why sometimes community groups do not work for some mothers and how this is processed or resolved within the group and among the members. Do they feel like an outgroup member within the group they are attending? Seppälä et al.'s (2022) study highlighted a way of evaluating three mothers' experiences and their "social exclusion" story type. The mothers actively attended various local groups and clubs for mothers and children but did not form close relationships with the other mothers. The new group memberships did not therefore efficiently support their adaptation to their life transition as new mothers. They also felt their experiences about new motherhood were not shared by other mothers, although they felt uncomfortable disclosing this in the group. However, the new group was not meaningless to them, and they engaged with it (at some level), as they kept participating in it. The interviews conducted as part of the study revealed a range of themes that are similar to the ones I have identified through working with groups. I have included some of the study's findings from the new mothers' responses to illustrate their experiences, and how these have been addressed with the groups I have researched as well as been actively engaged in.

> Rina was in her late 30s and a mother of a 9-month-old. She had proactively looked for the company by attending local clubs and events for mothers and children. However due to her infant having health problems she felt 'isolated' and like 'an outsider'. Her inability to share other mothers' experiences prevented her from really joining them.

> Teija was in her mid-30s and mother of a 9-month-old. She had just moved to the area and her pregnancy had been problematic. Therefore, she participated in formal peer support groups within social services, and local clubs. At the local clubs she stated no one else in that group talks about tiredness or depression or any other negative feelings of motherhood.

Furthermore, she experienced that the mothers did not want to talk about their difficult experiences or that they dwelt in an unrealistic 'baby bubble', into which Teija had difficulty entering. She also recounted how she had been rejected by other mothers and felt stigmatised when she had talked about her hard experiences.

Eveliina believed that socialising with other mothers and children was her duty as a mother, and she 'forced' herself to attend various local groups, clubs and events for mothers and children. Eveliina felt like she could not be herself among other mothers and she doubted their willingness to understand her imperfect motherhood.

These "social disconnection" story types offered in the article were defined by an even deeper disconnection from other mothers living in the area. The motherhood they perceived among others did not correspond to their understanding of how to be a mother, underlining their sense of alienation and disidentification with this potential new group. They rejected the version of motherhood identity that they believed other local mothers shared because it threatened the continuity of their own identity.

Another area was the purpose of the groups and why the mothers chose to opt in or out of the groups' experiences. In the study, the cost-benefit of attending was therefore considered. This was questioned by some mothers:

Essi was in her mid-30s and mother of an 8-month-old and felt that she did not need any new people in her life and that her young child did not need the company of other children either. She spent time with her old friends but had started to miss the company of local mothers when her child's rhythm had changed. Essi perceived that local mothers did not correspond to her goals and interests as an educated and well-off mother, and she considered that building social relations with other mothers demanded resources that she was unwilling to invest in these local mothers. Instead of building relations with local mothers during her maternity leave, she participated in networks and workshops that would support her career development.

Their findings revealed how the compatibility between old and new social identities can facilitate the gain of new group membership in the context of new motherhood. The possibility of realising pre-motherhood goals and interests with other mothers enabled the development of meaningful social relations. If the expectations of the other mothers threatened their participants' self-definitions, they disidentified with other mothers and chose to retain their personal identity rather than immerse themselves in the group and its social integration. It is, however, worth mentioning that some of the mothers who experienced disruption in their transition to motherhood and did not form close relationships with other local community mothers still routinely joined them. They continued to seek out company even if they experienced a fear of stigmatisation within the group. This suggests that the groups were not meaningless to them and that they even seemed to identify with them at some level. The findings also supported previous studies that groups can be limited when having children is the only commonality shared between them. Belonging to the common social category of "new mothers" may not be enough for the development of relational intimacy, although common experiences and similar understandings of motherhood can support the development of relational intimacy (Seppälä et al., 2021).

The forming of groups for new mothers and their purpose for social support

Social support is support that is considered to be functional, and which leads the receiver of the support to feel cared for, valued, and with a sense of belonging to a larger network. This support can therefore improve health and wellbeing by reducing stress levels among new mothers. As revealed in this chapter, social support may be provided by partners, family, peers, colleagues, and others within the community. Social support has been categorised into two main areas:

- structural support
- functional support.

Structural support refers to the existence and quantity of support through formal and informal social relationships, whereas functional support is the specific type of perceived support. This can include **emotional support** through understanding and the encouragement to express feelings, warmth, nurturance, and reassurance.

Functional support involves providing advice and guidance, helping others to understand, and sourcing resources and/

or coping strategies, information, advice, and management strategies.

In the groups I have worked with, I have often adopted a person-centred approach as a form of emotional support. This is a humanistic way of working and looks at the intrinsic motivations of the individual. As practitioners, the following three elements are core to navigating the parent relationship:

- Understanding – of a given situation and mindset
- Congruence – being open and honest in communication; and
- Empathy – not getting embroiled in emotions but appreciating situations and the emotions attached to them (Rogers, 1980).

Person-centred approaches are about discovering and acting on what is important to a person and what is important for them. It is about finding the right balance through a process of continual listening and learning. Listening helps to inform you about the parent's capacities and choices and to signpost necessary resources and services. Listening with intention as well as attention is important in creating a supportive relationship. It also gives voice to the parent so they do not feel ignored or silenced. Sharing power enables parents to work together and make choices rather than simply being informed by the group's facilitator. Personal construct theory is also a way of understanding the ideas that shape each person's individual lens on the world. As predictions are made in understanding external events, interpretations are made. Trying to understand new mothers' views of the world helps us to understand their perspectives and listen meaningfully.

Figure 4 Activities together

It has been argued that for social support to be effective, the support needs to be personalised, and needs must align with the support provided. Women, in times of stress, are more likely to give, access, and benefit from social support. In Dennis and Chung-Lee's (2006, p. 327) review, which included cross-cultural data on women up to one year postpartum, they reported that women wanted:

- To be given permission to talk in-depth about their feelings, including ambivalent and difficult feelings;
- To talk with a non-judgemental person who would spend time listening to them, take them seriously, and understand and accept them for who they are; and
- Recognition that there was a problem and reassurance that other mothers experience similar feelings and that they would get better.

With this in mind, examples of the micro stories about women's lived experiences in community groups will highlight the benefits to their personal identity, social identity, and sense of belonging.

Learning objective
Listening to new mothers

To understand the significance and benefits of listening to new mothers about their experiences and need to connect, as well as gaining a sense of belonging.

3

Mothers' virtual connections and in-person connections

Belonging as a social group and the value of connections

Chapter 3 moves on to the recent past and how mothers have been impacted by the pandemic and beyond. It focuses on how the nation moved towards virtual landscapes as a way of retaining and connecting new mothers who were physically isolated. The collective voice of a writing group for mothers reflects the power of belonging and empowerment as an individual as they live through an uncertain time and space. Reaching out and collaborative groups are considered, with belonging at the centre of the discussion.

The beginning

Odent (2001) states that childbirth can be challenging during caesarean operations, when a woman's "love hormones" are reduced, resulting in potential psychological consequences for the mother and their infant. Caesarean births may entail lower childbirth satisfaction and more concern about the condition of the child, as well as an increased risk of maternal depression. While we recognise all forms of childbirth may contribute to a mismatch between expectation and reality, there are arguments about increased vulnerability factors associated with issues during labour. It is a transition that can be overwhelming and emotionally challenging, requiring significant adjustment to lifestyles and relationships that women perhaps do not realise prior to the birth. Women may develop an unexpected mental illness during pregnancy or within the first year after giving birth. These can range from mild to severe. All these problems require attention, care, or treatment, from medical intervention to support in minimising the dripping tap of emotional mishandling and neglect in caring for their infant. When an infant is premature or born with additional health concerns, they may also require medical intervention. This can result in everyday challenges with infant care as well as causing anxiety among parents as they grieve for the infant they may have compared to the unknown reality of their baby being in special care and having an unknown future. The infant remaining in a special care unit may also influence the bonding between parents and their infant with the geographical distance between home and the hospital. The challenges of bonding may even have a long-term impact on the infant that is greater than that of their medical condition. So, in considering some of the issues associated with pregnancy, I wanted to include how a community group could be beneficial for new mothers during their pregnancy and afterwards. A type of group, I think, that has been beneficial and gained momentum since the pandemic is Maternal Journal groups, with the experience of the mothers being a huge part of their success and international growth.

During the pandemic and beyond: Experiences of connecting new mother during pregnancy

When I first heard about maternal journalling, I was training as an infant massage instructor and wanted to explore what types of community work were being carried out. I booked an online talk and was fortunate enough to be part of an introduction and then access the materials to begin a group myself. Many of the connections were online, and I think since the pandemic this has proved beneficial as a starting point to consider joining a group in person.

The Maternal Journal groups began in 2017 as a way of bringing creativity and connection to new mothers and birthing parents when they needed it most. The founder is a mother, artist, and midwife. On her community visits to see parents, she was struck by how many people had nowhere to process and share their new emotions and experiences. Working with a group of like-minded artists, she set up Maternal Journal to support people with a creative outlet and a friendly space for parents to meet and connect. Maternal Journal started out as workshops hosted by facilitators and now holds groups internationally with an online community. Maternal Journal is now a global community movement and offers a series of creative workshops and techniques to support parents throughout the transitions, joys, and challenges of pregnancy, birth, and parenthood. In developing the workshop series, the organisers have worked with artists, therapists, doulas, and friends in creating innovative ways for participants to use their journalling resources each week. There are resources so that each session has an activity that can be made for the journal. These range from styles including poetry and prose writing to drawing and painting. Each session is organised with an activity introduced and facilitated by the lead. The groups' purpose is to provide an inclusive and safe space for anyone who has experienced pregnancy, given birth, or identifies as a mother or as a woman or non-binary carer. A typical group comprises pregnant women, birthing people, and mothers and usually has between 6 and 12 members. The group meet for a few hours together at a regular time. Each session is guided by a different journalling exercise to encourage exploration of creativity, emotions, and experiences. A group is normally facilitated by a midwife, birth worker, mental health professional, or experienced workshop leader. Emotive feelings can emerge during the group workshops, and the groups are not recommended for people with a history of severe mental illness (www.maternaljournal.org/guiding-principles).

In 2018, Laura Godfrey-Isaacs posted in *Birth, Art & Culture* about the success of maternal journalling, and some of the experiences the participants shared on the website are quoted here to illustrate the community and belonging developed:

> I feel energised and given permission and support to continue to find and establish my own space and voice creatively, at home and outside. This, in turn, makes me feel already less anxious and fearful about the impact of

this baby on my sanity. Like I will have more tools at my disposal, should I feel myself teetering on the edge of depression again. The other aspect which I hugely value is how openly political it is, how different and broad the range of women, but all united, I think, in seeing and talking openly about how political motherhood and female mental health and work are. I find this such a relief and support.

(parent, n.d.)

The weekly workshops are totally the highlight of my week: they're fresh, different, so far away from my every day, so relevant to my life currently and exactly what I need. I'm loving being introduced to the artists and trying out things I wouldn't have done on my own initiative. It's inspiring and energy giving.

(parent, n.d.)

The Maternal Journal as a concept and a working model is fantastic. I've found the past two sessions joyous, cathartic, hopeful, inspiring and informative. I feel blessed to have access to such a brilliant group.

(parent, n.d.)

Creating the artwork itself was both cathartic and therapeutic. I felt valued as a pregnant woman.

(parent, n.d.).

Keeping a maternal journal has been a very helpful and positive experience. I think it's contributed to my continued mental stability.

(All4Maternity, 2023)

Having a focus and being creative seemed to bring something out, rather than the group of pregnant women coming together and reflecting on their week, clothing, and their pending birth or experience of birth. Rather, it feels that by doing certain journalling, it goes deeper and allows a space for the women to explore their inner selves and reflections beyond the everyday experiences they had. I do remember that although I hadn't attended the group, I had decided to complete some art projects I had let stagnate for several years. This focus on being creative certainly helped me through some challenging days and nights where I felt overwhelmed and unable to cope during the last month of pregnancy and even more during the first few weeks after giving birth. I did attend an online art group and accessed sessions, but I think the journalling group, either in person or virtual, would have been beneficial in not just meeting other mothers but also exploring and accepting how I felt as a new parent as being OK and that I was good enough.

After birth

During and after birth, infants continue to completely depend on their carer, although it is a mistake to think they are helpless beings. Rather, I consider infants to be active agents with many fast-developing abilities and with a growing consciousness about their care, in whatever shape that care is offered. Gopnik (2016) argues that the search for the correct techniques in rearing and caring for an infant is pointless and concludes that relationships are far more complex than a set of consciously manipulated variables, as childcare experts often insist they are. However, ensuring there is secure attachment and availability of carers is thought to underpin the long-term healthy development of infants, whether this is one or serval carers. The carers, often the mother or the adult regularly parenting, become attuned to their infant's emotions at least some of the time. In a secure, consistent, and stable environment, an infant will gain independence and a sense of themselves in their surroundings.

The influence of the pandemic on these families

Attachment and bonding are generally considered to be an essential part of parenting and although culturally this has been argued to be perpetuating a monotropic relationship, for many parents, this is reality, particularly in the west, and the mother is often considered to be the primary carer in the first few months. While I am not arguing that that there is one relationship that is more important than all the rest, as the concept of monotropy suggests, I do think culturally, and specifically in the UK, the mother is generally, though not always, the main carer in the first few months. So, in consideration of this, what happens when society has shaped this form of care and then an unprecedented pandemic happens? For many mothers, this meant being isolated, unaccompanied by loved ones during the birth, and then expected to parent their infant, with online meetings with health professionals and in the absence of support from family and friends that would normally have been part of their community. In understanding the value of community groups, I wanted to highlight the power of the online group during this time and how virtual meetings became a lifeline for many new mothers with little in-person support and comfort. The reality was of mothers being physically alone with their infant, but in some cases struggling with the bonding experience, which is often assumed as an inevitable consequence in the monotropic relationship.

Mothership Writers group

The Mothership Writers group was one group that highlighted the strengths of being connected during the 2020 pandemic. Emylia Hart is the author of four novels, including one bestseller, as well as a creative writing teacher. The Mothership Writers group was developed because of her own lived experiences as a mother and a writer. She stated, as a novelist, that she is familiar with framing the events of her life in a narrative, and with seeing personal experience as potentially rich creative territory. She also advocated that the benefits of writing are not just for the few who are creative but are there for all. She developed the group with an introduction for members initially to link through a paper, whether fiction or fact, believing this can be therapeutic, empowering, and fun.

Hart has offered over 150 workshops for Mothership Writers, creating a space for new mothers, connecting creativity and maternity, and currently continues to do so with the community building.

However, this group's activities during lockdown is what I want to highlight. During 2020, I came across this group when exploring mothers' writing and new mothers' experience. I had read some national policy-driven reports as well as charity reports about the need for more support, highlighting the need to foster maternal mental health. During this time, I was contributing to some research and felt that I wanted to reflect not just on what was needed for new mothers in society as a collective but also their lived experiences in shaping what was needed.

The responses Hart obtained from her workshops during the pandemic culminated in a report titled *Born in Lockdown*, with 277 authors and one shared experience: becoming a new mother in 2020. The mothers were already attending the virtual groups and wanted to collaborate and share their voice about the realities of new motherhood during this time. The coronavirus pandemic intensified what was already a challenging time for many, making the need for self-expression even more vital. The letters together aimed to tell the story of what it was like to navigate new motherhood in 2020. The letters reflected the diversity of mothers' experiences, the complexity, and their conflicts as much as the joy and wonder. In terms of participation, there were no selection criteria, apart from having had a child in the past two years, and anyone who wanted to participate could be included.

The process was that participants were asked to write in fragments, each comprising no more than a handful of connecting sentences, perhaps 50 words. They could be scribbled down during their night feed, or recorded as a voice note during the night or while out walking. This culminated in a free flow of thoughts and free writing exercises, allowing moments to be captured that otherwise might be lost, inaccessible, or edited for meaning at a later time. There was no brief, with the mothers empowered to lead as a collective. The collection published reflected the diversity of mothers' experiences, the complexity, and their conflicts as much as the joy and wonder. In analysing the report, I have themed the mothers' experiences and how as a group they reflected on aspects of care and being part of a virtual group and their issues around belonging and community.

Their voices in sharing the experience as a collective

Food and drink

> It is 19 March 2020. It is chaos. My baby is a day old. He will not latch. I am drowning in the heat of the post-natal ward. The shops are sold out of formula. I want nothing more than to go home and to stay there for the next three months. My timeline is filled with videos of doorstep clapping. It reminds me that it's Thursday. I look around the dimly lit post-natal ward to see midwives and cleaning staff expertly doing their rounds. Hot tears plop down my cheeks. My baby's here and we're both OK. It's all OK.
>
> (parent in Hall, 2021)

> Baby brain isn't what they said. It's actually mother brain. MB is multi-tasking one handed, eyes on a baby, a cat, planning meals, sleeps, walks, things to buy today, tomorrow, next month for the baby, the house, others. Mother brains are incredible, and I am holding more than ever.
>
> (parent in Hall, 2021)

Pre-birth lifestyle

> My eldest is having to isolate due to a confirmed case at nursery. Really though, how can I entertain a pre-schooler

and a baby, all day, every day, shut away? I'm glad they won't remember days like these. I hope I don't either.

(parent in Hall, 2021)

The world's wonders are empty, hospitals are full. Play parks closed, with tape, like a crime scene. Our bed is full but so are our hearts. Tired eyes explore your perfect, tiny, soft face. Your eyes flicker open. You smile as you watch the light dance away the shadows.

(parent in Hall, 2021)

Community: A village

It takes a village… I wish I could see mine. I'm aching, leaking, bleeding and oh so very tired. Anxiety gnaws away at my groggy, hormone-saturated mind. You are like a little milk limpet and I cling to you in return. We'll get through this my girl, we have to.

(parent in Hall, 2021)

It takes a village to raise a baby, I read somewhere. Where's my village, I wondered? Feeling so removed from everything today. Even your baby giggles can't penetrate a certain greyness. It's like this month, November. You're playing on the floor and I'm writing these lines, crying. I wonder how many other mums are out there, like me at the moment. And that made me feel a bit less alone, but not any less sad.

(parent in Hall, 2021)

As the second lockdown was announced my heart sank. The small, trusted support network I'd managed to build would no longer to be able to help me at home and I feared my mental health would spiral again being stuck indoors alone with an unsettled baby and difficult toddler.

(parent in Hall, 2021)

They say it takes a village to raise a child, but where do you turn when the village is closed? The usual support is deemed "unsafe". You have no choice but to dig deep inside, trusting that you were made for the role of being a mother. You focus on that bond between you and your baby, you realise that this is your most important life's work and that nothing is more precious than this child.

(parent in Hall, 2021)

Before we could even begin to build our village, we were banished to a wilderness with no map, no guide, no stars in the sky to tell us where to go. We were suddenly a three, bound tightly and fearfully together with love, like a bedroll.

(parent in Hall, 2021)

Creating themes for analysis of the extracts revealed more nuanced ways of writing during contemporary times. Texts, emails, online messages, and even vlogs have all widened the discursive spaces through which women can communicate (www.mother shipwriters.com/borninlockdown). This is evidenced with the mother writers asked to write in fragments, each comprising "no more than a handful of connecting sentences". I thought the way they spoke about the isolation and the lack of the community during this time really captured the power of the groups and the need for social interaction. The virtual group offered some solace but ultimately the physicality of the group was much needed for support during the early experiences of motherhood.

Choi et al. (2005) also highlighted that there is often a popular image of "happy families" that has been specifically mentioned by women as unrealistic in previous studies, with many even reporting feelings of anger at having been cheated and conned by this myth of motherhood. I found that some parallels could be drawn between Choi et al. (2005) and the new mothers in the study during the pandemic.

> When I [pause] when she was first born [pause] the crying actually made me feel desperately ill. Desperately ill. If she cried, I just felt like I wanted to [pause] give up, you know? Really, I mean honestly, I've thought some terrible things [pause] towards myself, not towards her.
>
> (parent in Hall (2021))

Another element of the ideology of motherhood that was also found to be a myth was that women should immediately be able to take care of their babies. The sub-theme of expectations of motherhood showed how the women overwhelmingly reported being unprepared for motherhood when their first child was born. For one woman, it was a "tremendous shock":

> …before I had Andrew I had no experience whatsoever with children, no experience whatsoever with babies… then all of a sudden I had this little baby you know to

look after and at three weeks he was screaming the place down and I didn't know what it was.

I'd never changed a nappy. I'd never, I'd never bottle fed a baby, I'd never looked after a baby… I didn't know what to do… I was in despair…

(parent in Hall, 2021)

These experiences were documented in 2005 and highlight that in 2020 the despair continued and heightened during the pandemic.

I do remember being on social media during the pandemic, and there were a few new mothers asking for support and advice. I recall talking to a couple of new mothers about their multiple births and although I never met them, I physically spoke to them regularly online and tried to reassure them that they were OK and that what they were experiencing was not unusual. I just felt like I had to reach out, reflecting on how I felt during my experience ten years earlier and how I would have managed without being able to go out and engage with others in groups and family. I felt it was a desperate time and underscored how motherhood is defined in the community and society in which I live.

Women's expectations, both in Choi et al. (2005) and in my experience, are strongly influenced by the myth of motherhood, with a lack of alternative motherhood discourses for women to draw on in constructing their own experiences. It is hardly surprising, therefore, that conflict occurs because of the discrepancy between the myth and the reality. It is almost a dichotomy of success or failure with little in-between as new motherhood is experienced.

In addition to feelings of inadequacy, women also felt that they should be able to cope with caring for a new baby, as well as domestic tasks and caring for others. This reflects the cultural representations of femininity today that are of a "superwoman" able to cope with so many competing demands. Women are reluctant to be seen to have failed as perhaps this would threaten their sense of self and their identity as a woman. As this is informed by discourses of femininity, femininity is performed by not revealing their true feelings and taking up the discourses of the perfect woman who can cope and who does not need help. I certainly recall feeling this and give an example of a group I attended and how I felt during this time.

I had just had twins and, having two other children, felt that after four months of ill health and caring for them that I ought to be trying to stimulate them more and offer more play opportunities. One of the issues I had was that I also had a 14-month-old and a four-year-old child. Therefore, trying to do anything practically at the weekend was challenging, and attending groups was something I felt I couldn't do. I had already made myself unwell trying to maintain the home, and my partner did not seem to be coping, drifting in and out of work and being supportive at selective times, but often preferring the order of employment to home during this time. I decided to contact a sing and sign group that I had previously attended, and the facilitator welcomed all four children. The group was small, and I was able to attend weekly. I was also only charged for one child, and this financial support was a relief and encouraged me to attend regularly. It was an organised group and there was a plan for the session. We did a welcome song, songs together, and then free-flow songs with puppets. I was able to share these at home. The group was intended for my one-year-old although my older child knew the songs too and could join in. I think during this time making the effort to attend was hard, and I felt self-conscious coming into a room with four children and overwhelming the space. One of the ways I felt connected was that I was already known by the group. The other main motivation to attend was that the facilitator allowed me to share how I felt and held an emotional space for me. She didn't rush me and would always welcome me. Some mornings had been hard, and this was group I could carve out time to attend and be partly myself as well as enjoying the time with the children.

This community group experience was so powerful that I then went on to research the value of emotional connections through baby signing and song. I was immersed in how connections to finger movements and touch could be so significant. Through attending a community group, I felt empowered and found solace that although I was exhausted for most of the time, I could reflect on a positive experience and the benefits of the group. This experience motivated me to think about how other mothers feel as well and in what forms of groups they may find acceptance and belonging too.

Learning objective
The value of connections and belonging

The value of connections and belonging with an understanding about virtual community groups could be developed and facilitated, as well as approaches that could be helpful in creating a productive virtual community group.

4

Contemporary community care

Nurturing narratives between mothers and their infants within an infant massage and singing group

After a return to a new normal and a national shift in funding, this chapter focuses on groups offered to mothers within and beyond the criteria of being eligible to access free support in the community. From mental health to physical challenges, the groups within local authority centres enable new mothers to access free spaces and groups that enhance a sense of belonging and connectivity. As a facilitator of the groups, the author reflects on what it meant to her when she was a new mother, as well as for new mothers today, and the narratives shared about what the group means to them as they embark on infant massage classes.

The value of touch

In 1948, Halliday (Hayward, 2009) made the link between mortality in infants and touch, noting that infants who were deprived of maternal bodily contact were more inclined to lose appetite and would waste away, resulting in death. Subsequently, volunteers were brought in and encouraged to attend children's hospitals as a way of providing fretful and vulnerable infants with regular cuddles, handling and rocking them. The comfort the infants received led to a steady decline in mortality rates. Montagu (1986) also emphasised that human skin is the largest and most sensitive of our organs, offering us protection and the earliest channel of communication. However, many parents and professionals caring for infants fear being accused of inappropriate touch, and the discourses can be overwhelmingly about the reduction of needing to touch beyond the physical handling of infants rather than encouraging a healthy touch approach. Therefore, my position is concerned with promoting healthy touch as a source of comfort and emotional regulation, and a medium through which we communicate and learn. It seems to have a particular potency when combined with other senses, which appears pertinent to our understanding of the function of infant massage.

Valuing touch goes further back in history to a time when the primary concern was the influence of professionals advocating a strict regime of not picking up the infant, feeding to the clock, and focusing on physical health. There remained a concern that although clinical, sterilised environments were perceived as high-quality environments, infant mortality remained high. Warmer mothering approaches, with infants being carried, cooed to, and given the sensory experience of the skin, yielded positive results. Klaus and Kennell (1995) also evaluated that the maternal sensitive period was shortly after birth because this period was important for bonding to occur, which is not unique to the mother but also involves other family members. Therefore, practices such as kangaroo care, skin-to-skin contact between parent or sibling from birth, are valuable and contradict the often-hands-off approach that for so many years was advocated in a bid to ensure healthcare was optimum. We now know touch and handling are important, especially when newborns are attached to machinery and have tubes inserted for their physical survival. Kangaroo care comforts and soothes infants, particularly preterm infants. The infants are warm, and they have regular heart rates and respiration. They sleep more deeply and cry less. For the carers, the skin-to-skin contact, according to Stern et al. (1995), encourages breastfeeding and bonding with their newborn.

As a mother, I reflect on when my daughter was in a special unit after birth for a few weeks because she was premature. When I saw her in the incubator, I was quite frightened and thought if I cuddled her, I might pull out one of the tubes or knock something. With gentle reassurance from the nurse practitioner, I was able to sit carefully in a chair and hold her to me for a few hours. The nurse practitioner on the ward gently unclipped the tubes and passed her to me. She responded to questions and helped but then moved away and allowed me time to hold my daughter. I will never forget the feeling of happiness, observing her in my trembling hands. It helped me initiate a bond with her, and I felt more confident to care for her when we got home a few weeks later. It was during this time that I began to seek out other forms of community groups, and the health visitor asked if I would be interested in attending an infant massage programme for six weeks that the care assistant was leading. I was happy to attend and wanted to know more about infant massage.

Infant massage was introduced to western countries by practitioners including Amelia Auckett and Vimala McClure, who both spent periods of time in India. Infant massage programmes offered in western countries today incorporate both Indian and Swedish massage techniques, although there is no standardisation of the infant massage routine or national regulation of massage facilitators. Among the range of programmes available, there is noticeable variation in techniques and emphasis. The International Association of Infant Massage (IAIM) was founded by Vimala McClure in the USA and was the first such global organisation, albeit that massage has existed for centuries in many countries around the world. Vimala McClure was the first person to put together a professional programme after travelling to India and observing the deprivation but also the nurturing connection and touch between mothers and their infants living there as she ventured through the streets. The theory, curriculum, and focus are unique and have been carefully developed and refined through research and practical experience since its inception in 1976. The IAIM symbolises the unity of people seeking to support nurturing touch between parents and infants. It strives to support parents in creating a nurturing environment for themselves and their child. The purpose of the IAIM is to promote nurturing touch and communication through training, education, and research so that parents, caregivers, and children are loved, valued, and respected throughout the whole community (www.iaim.org.uk).

As the infant massage course discusses, Thomas and Chess (1977) identified three core temperaments in infants.

- Easy infants are very easy-going and develop regular eating and sleeping patterns with ease.
- Difficult infants tend to be very emotional, irritable, and fussy, and cry a lot. They also tend to have irregular eating and sleeping patterns.
- Slow-to-warm-up infants have a low activity level and tend to withdraw from new situations and people. They are slow to adapt to new experiences but accept them after repeated exposure.

For me, this extends to how the infants feel during the day and night, and all these aspects can be observed depending on whether they need feeding, sleep, or stimulation. The more apparent temperament can play a significant role in terms of influencing how the infant responds to their environment. What is particularly important is the degree of "fit" between the infant's temperament and the environment into which they are born. For example, an infant who is "difficult" and born to a first-time mother who is experiencing post-natal depression is considered at an increased likelihood of poor outcomes because of the poor fit between their high level of need and their mother's inability to meet that need. Infant massage can help this relationship and has also been used with women in vulnerable circumstances and who are engaged in recovery programmes (Porter et al., 2015). Hahn et al. (2016) also undertook a qualitative study with 13 infant-mother dyads with the aim of developing an enhanced understanding of how infant massage may influence infant-carer relationships and infant behaviours. Empowerment, enjoyment, calm, and comfort were the key themes that emerged from infant massage, supporting the infant-carer attachment. In a recent review of massage research, Field (2014) claimed that massage had demonstrated positive effects with prenatal depression, for premature and full-term infants, and in relation to autism, pain management, immune conditions, and issues associated with ageing. Furthermore, Field (2014) claimed that moderate, as opposed to light, pressure massage was key to ensuring positive effects, such as weight gain in preterm infants. In recognising this, the infant's massage is intended to align to the rhythms of the infant's temperament rather than when the parent wants to do the massage.

A massage routine can be used when physical problems like tummy pain, gas, constipation, or colic occur, and is done at a separate time to the regular massage.

When an infant is relaxed but alert is a good time for infant massage in the group. Observing and recognising temperament during the day can also help reframe how we interpret crying and emotional behaviour and the reasons for behaviours. Knowing infants' temperaments helps in supporting infants in ways that respect their individual differences, working with the infants rather than trying to change them. During the infant massage, one of the key principles in the group is to encourage asking permission.

The "ritual" of asking permission will be done once at the beginning of the massage. Facilitators are encouraged to remember that asking permission is a continual process throughout the massage group session. This process involves watching cues and pausing at each new area to be massaged,

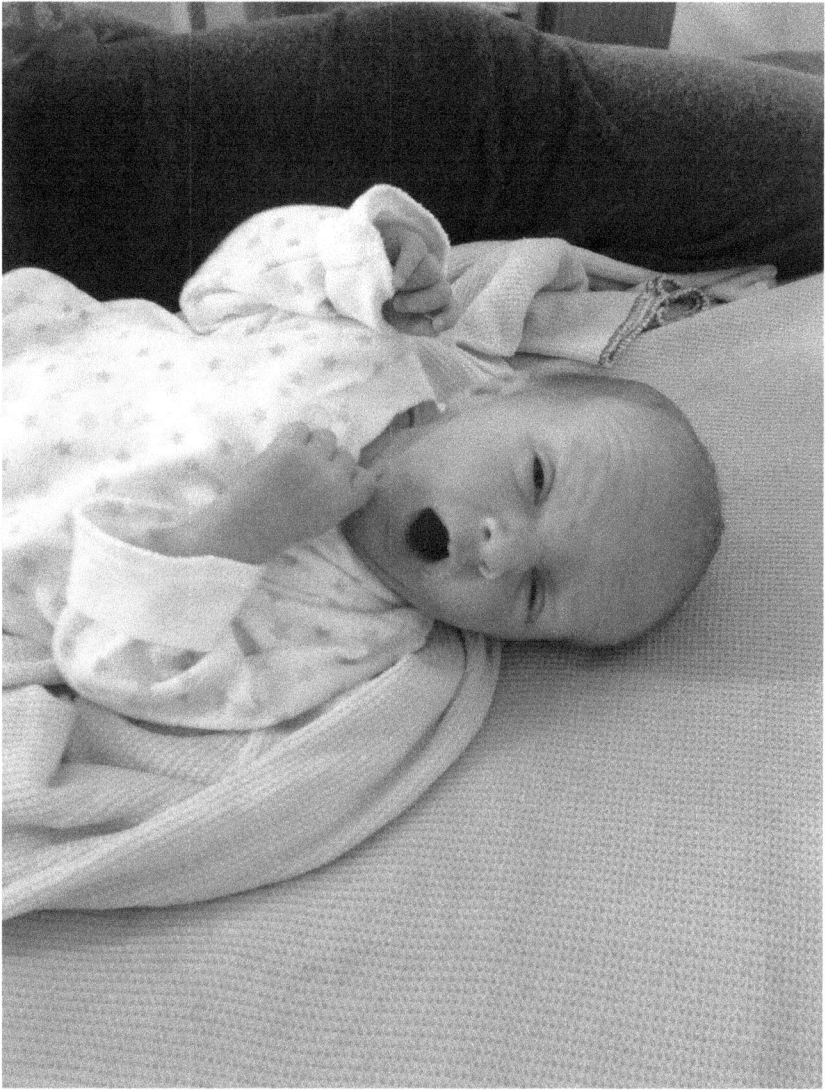

Figure 5 Infant massage

making sure the infant is receptive to continuing with massage. Infant massage can therefore offer families a special environment focusing on the infant-carer connection, and offering important respite from the challenges that may disrupt the development

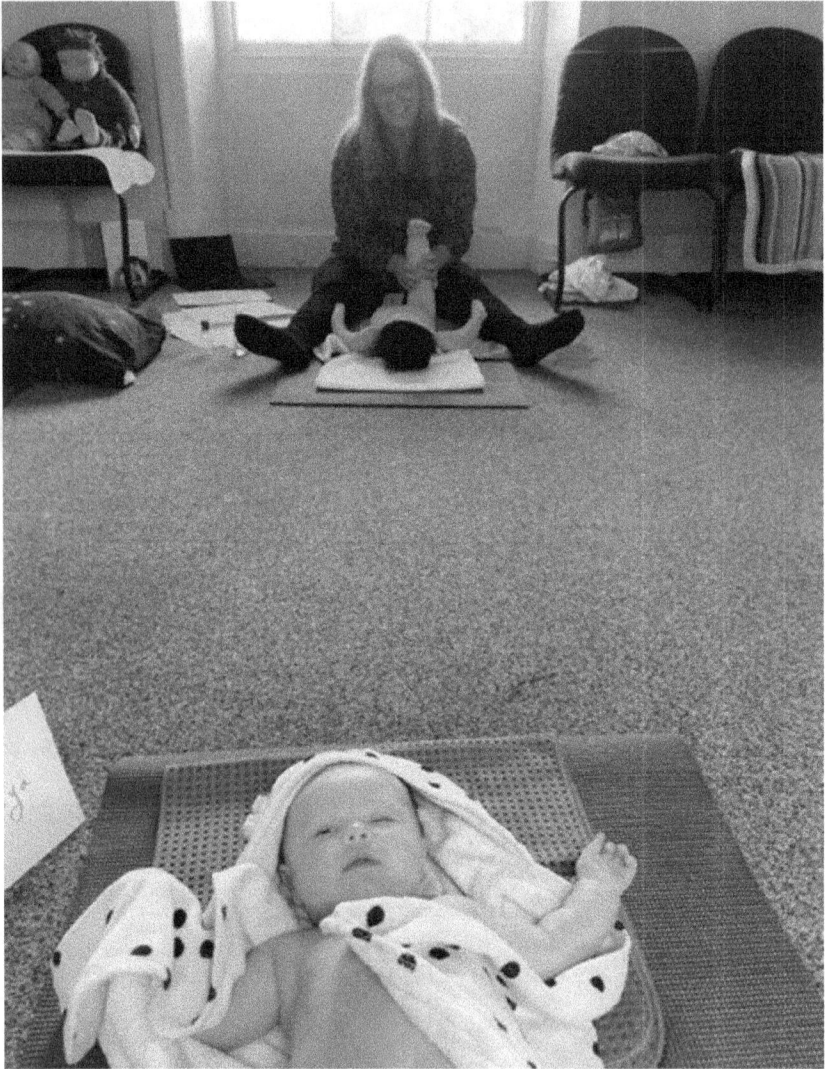

Figure 6 Alert and resting

of this connection. However, the environments surrounding the families, and the timing of the programme were found to be critical; the massage context needs to support infant and carer feelings of containment (Bion, 1962) and regulation (Gerhardt, 2004) as they adjust to a new life phase.

A personal experience of infant massage

It was a cold morning and I had rushed to collect things together ready to begin my session of infant massage. The health visitor had recommended it, and I felt I ought to try it as a way of connecting with my infant and relaxing. I parked at an unfamiliar venue and managed to grab my bag and infant and went into the building. I was directed upstairs and entered what was quite a spacious room and was invited to take a seat on the floor by a mat. I found an area and was able to get ready, and I put my daughter down. She was awake and quite content. I smiled at her as I anticipated instructions. One by one, more parents arrived. A few had arrived with partners although predominantly the room was filled with mothers and their infants. There were about 15 in total, and we all had a mat to sit by. The facilitator welcomed us all and explained the session. By this point, there was already lots of noise coming from parents quietly talking to each other or their infant gurgling or crying. Some parents looked a little anxious as they listened to the instructions.

We were encouraged to relax and listen to our infant, and I felt fortunate that I could be quite confident that my infant was going to be fairly quiet as I had already noted she was relaxed. This was very different from my older son! She was also very responsive, and this helped me tune in to her needs, stopping and resting when she had had enough. I observed her kicking her legs and her facial expressions. When she was happy for me to continue with the stroke, I stroked her legs and checked she was flat on the mat.

Some of the other mothers seemed quite preoccupied with the worry that their infant was going to be difficult or soil, so they had a nappy ready, having been encouraged to remove them during the massage. A few infants didn't seem comfortable, and the mothers stood up and rocked them, walking around the room as they cried.

At the end of each week's session, we had space to discuss how the week had gone, although this was quite brief. I spoke to a few parents during the six weeks of attending, although I didn't exchange numbers with anyone. I thought there was lots of small talk with some of the parents being first-time mums, and they spoke about feeding or sleep time. Having a second child, I felt somehow a little more removed from the interactions. I was quite shy but had also had a challenging pregnancy, and because my daughter was not what I considered difficult, I didn't feel I had much to offer. She ate well, slept, and enjoyed interacting with her brother and myself.

One of the key things I did note was that the process of physical touch involved in the session made me slow down. I was always busy and now reflect that even though I enjoyed caring for my daughter, it was always at a faster pace than I had realised. In taking the time to talk to her, make eye contact, and initiate physical touch, I realise how much slower I was and how this was benefiting her. I did share time with the other mothers next to me, and they agreed it was easier to automatically carry out nappy changing or feeding without much thought about the experience. Previously, I had been very automatic, and the benefit of massage for me was slowing down and enjoying the interaction as much as my daughter. The massage was a bonding experience and one I could repeat at home in the evenings.

Some of the strokes were discussed quite quickly, and I don't recall much about health benefits for my daughter, such as a reduction in wind or other physical benefits. I noticed by week three that some parents were not present and wondered if these were the infants who hadn't settled. A few infants who had cried during the first session didn't return and at least two skipped some of the weeks. I think concerns about hurting the infants were mentioned, although this was something I didn't find challenging. One of the key ideas was that if the infant slept or cried then we would stop massaging. A few parents didn't remove their clothes either, probably worried they might get too cold. However, I also noted many looked to each other for reassurance, and if we were unsure of what to do, we would often take our lead from what others were doing, rather than asking.

Quite a few parents knew each other because they had been referred by the health visitor and so were already attending a group together. This changed the dynamic of the group considerably. I'm not sure if it was because I was slightly older or because I didn't know anyone, but I didn't get a sense of belonging.

For me, the motivation was to enjoy spending some time with my daughter and learning something new with her. I didn't feel a sense of community with the other mothers, and because there wasn't time for prolonged informal conversations, it was very much like attending an appointment. However, I must have sensed something in terms of group connection because I attended each session and do recall looking forward to attending.

I would have liked some small further connections with the other mothers though.

My experience as an instructor facilitating an infant massage group

Working with infants, I decided to train to be an infant massage instructor with the IAIM. Once trained, I organised my first sessions with a group of mums. The advice was to have a maximum of eight mums and so, for me, six seemed to be a good number to start with as a facilitator. I expected some absences, but they all arrived. I spent the first few minutes asking them about their infants and what they wanted to share. The prompt questions were intended to start conversations among the attendees. As a facilitator, it wasn't my role to lead and advise, but rather to create a space for everyone to develop a voice and listen to each other.

There were seven mothers, and no fathers attended. They often came a few minutes early and took their time to settle. During the first week, one of the mothers was very apologetic about her infant crying, saying she felt that she didn't like it, meaning the massage. I told her not to worry and said that she could just feed her infant or settle with her. She wasn't very relaxed, and because her infant was quite a bit younger than the others, I wonder if she was feeling more anxious in comparison. The other six mothers had also previously had a child, and they were able to share anecdotes and compare their past experiences, which may have contributed to the first-time mother's anxiety. I was able to talk to her in the break, but I think she was feeling overwhelmed at that time. Over the following weeks, a core group of five regularly attended, and they would go for coffee at a nearby café after sessions. They particularly enjoyed the talking and having a space to ask each other for advice about the infant equipment they were buying and other places they had been to. There was a thread of confidence among them as they were second-time mothers, but they also appreciated the current unique situation they were in. They would also try to look at their infant and talk to them while I was leading the strokes. I always had an infant massage doll and didn't massage the infants themselves. I made an effort to be the role model and use the appropriate language to promote bonding, highlighting permission and respect, so they could observe how to do this with their own infant. A couple of topics were regularly discussed, and these were sleep tiredness and growth of the infant. It was interesting to see that health was the priority, and I think that was probably unsurprising because most of the infants attending were around 10–14 weeks old. This also connected to who else they met regularly, which was officially the health visitor.

Supporting recommended groups

When I led subsequent groups at different venues, there were more interactions, more variations in the group, and more cultural diversity. There were more international mothers attending, and this other group often included mothers who spoke about home topics. This included where they could visit or when they were visiting their family at home. Extended family members also increasingly came to this group, as well as partners regularly. Each group was held at various venues, and I felt this impacted on who would attend, irrespective of the topics discussed among them.

A deeper connection and opportunities to share their anxieties were ways of reducing their isolation. I also think, similar to my own experiences, that because it was more a social gathering and similar to the maternal journalling previously discussed, they were actively doing something. It felt like a purposeful group to attend, and a feeling of solidarity developed in the group. While they were gaining a feeling of belonging and continuity, they were also doing something. The infant strokes were worthwhile for their infants because some of the mothers felt they were able to relieve their infant's colic or wind as well. They often continued the strokes at home in their own space as well. One mother said she had practised the strokes and carried them out during the evening routine and felt this was helping to develop a richer and more rewarding relationship between her son and herself.

As a facilitator, I was able to observe changes within the infants each week and how the mothers changed in their role. Generally, some felt increasingly relaxed and gained confidence while others seemed to be developing a more authentic persona, recognising and sharing how tired they felt or how challenged they were by coping as a new mother. The group facilitated a sharing connection, where empathy, listening, and positive regard became the principles of the group.

A community of practice with referred parents

Individuals learn by a process together rather than assimilating what they are told. By constructing knowledge, the process is modelled and supported in the surrounding community the member is immersed in.

To create the community of practice, three dimensions of a group are considered to be necessary:

- What the group is about: what is being planned and discussed;
- How it functions: does everyone have a voice and how are roles distributed; and
- What capability it has produced (Wenger, 1998): following through with activities and practices and then reflecting back on its successes and challenges.

The collaborative relationship of learning together also has benefits in terms of creating social support and reducing stress. If less experienced or confident members feel supported, good self-esteem is evident and developed. Clough and Corbett (2001) suggest learning is linked to experiences, with people's analytical thinking about their experiences put into practice. This can be illustrated with activities drawing on different modes such as listening to each other.

However, developing a community of practice is not without anxiety and tension, and there are inevitably going to be issues to resolve for harmony to occur (Garvey, 2009). Wenger (1998) believed tensions often exist as a way of keeping personal thinking hidden or when an individual is unsure or lacks confidence. Through creating open discussions about constraints and possible issues, a sense of community is created (Seifert and Mandzuk, 2006).

I noticed this when I attended a community-run sensory class. The sensory sessions were organised to provide ideas for creative play, tummy time, movement, visual development, textures, scents, and music in simple and practical ways through song and games that could be easily repeated at home. A range of songs and rhymes were used to develop early speech and language skills, and sensory signing activities aided the babies in communicating from birth. Resources were brought and shared by the centre, and there was a voluntary cost for a cold drink.

The classes were held in a social services building, and funding had been received so local parents could access the six-week course with their infants. Typically, the course was privately run and therefore inaccessible to many parents who would have been financially challenged by attending. By creating this opportunity, the local health visitor had recommended the class to parents. While this was beneficial, there was initially some stigma around this, and some mothers would openly challenge what was offered or disengage partway through the session. They were recommended to turn off their mobile phones, but some continued to access them during the session. There was a sense of being grateful for attending, but for some also a fear of feeling they were perceived as a "needing the service", and this caused some anxiety. Questions were asked, and discussions around the motivation to attend the class were raised and shared with each other. In sharing some challenging conversations about coping and needing support, the identity of the group began to emerge, and the mothers began to engage more. They seemed to relax into the session and, knowing the pattern of the session, were more tuned in to the expectations and reduced their time disengaging and being on their mobiles.

Boundaries and tensions were therefore openly discussed and worked through by coming together and reflecting on experiences. Through reflective practice and a community, a sense of identity and engagement occurred.

Wenger (1998) recognised that knowledge was a key asset in building a community of learning and practice. He believed knowledge fulfilled several functions, including nodes for exchange for communities to become successful and develop. He drew on the following themes where knowledge can enhance a sense of community:

- Self-reflecting;
- Retaining knowledge in living ways: being aware and making sense of each other as a collective group; and
- Homes for identities: recognising and celebrating individual differences.

Learning objective
Models of connected community groups

To think about models of connected community groups and how these have been successful and what it might mean to establish social identity and belonging with new mothers and their infants.

5

New mothers and circles and spiritual groups

In moving forward since the pandemic, there has been a revival of women seeking solidarity and connection beyond the formal and mainstream organisations offered in society. Many new mothers seeking something less commercialised than baby showers but also wanting to celebrate the impending birth and arrival of their infant have found alternative practices with a focus on their spiritual meanings. Women's circles within and beyond the western view of religious practices have culminated in many women seeking and offering mother blessings and naming ceremonies rather than baptisms. The author reflects on her experiences where the community of connection and individual choice is part of the ceremony. In building a mother circle, there is a connection to the earth, and thanks to each, a space to reveal and be accepted in the here and now. As a group, this is a timely chapter in what the future may offer and hold for mothers if they choose.

Rituals and belonging

Studying rituals around pregnancy and welcoming the infant provides a deeper understanding beyond a medical and procedural approach. In western, secular societies, ritualising birth, such as through the baby shower, gender reveal, or party for the baby, is increasingly popular, although similar events have existed for many years in various societies. These are all emerging and renewed rituals associated with transitioning to parenthood. Some have connections to generational rituals like religious celebrations and gatherings of extended families. I am going to discuss these rituals where individuals come together as part of a community group, symbolically enacted during the ceremonies, and confirm that the pregnant mother and the newborn are acknowledged by their social group. Initially, the mother's blessing is when a pregnant woman and the foetus are both in a state of transition, with the mother's blessing revealing notions of the community and an equal, temporal, cohesive sense of togetherness between mother and baby (King, 1993).

Mother's blessing

Burns (2015) revealed the female community is an important element in this ritual. A Blessingway ceremony, more frequently known in the west as a mother's blessing, involves a circle of women (and men too) sharing, celebrating, and empowering the pregnant mother as she prepares for birth and motherhood. Fellow women including relatives and friends are present for empowerment in the group. They are all there to encourage and bless the journey to motherhood. It is the support from the mother's "tribe" as they embark on the parenting journey.

While it is a ceremony rather than a community group, the two coincide as women come together to share their experiences. It therefore symbolises the love and support being offered and can be considered to be a deep and transformational experience. It is also about sharing and celebrating, with the intention of blessing the mother and baby and feeling "held" and supported by those that love and respect her.

As a mother, I chose a mother's blessing, creating an informal event led by friends. It was an opportunity to acknowledge the birth beyond organised religion, with the process and event organised and managed in a fluid way rather than in the procedural baptism. Food and celebration were key, but it was also a way of recognising and giving thanks for a successful high-risk birth. A sense of belonging and connecting with others is then achieved. The ceremony ritual is designed to provide a deeply meaningful experience for the mother. The focus is honouring the mother's own belief system. The mother's blessing ceremony originated from the Navajo tradition, although each ceremony is unique, with some ceremonies including rituals from other cultures. According to Wyman (1971) in Navajo mythology, the Navajo word *nizho'ni'* is translated as beautiful and is a blessing across the life course. The ancient ritual is from the indigenous people of North America', who viewed it as the second blood rite for a woman, with her first being her first menstruation (Sturme, 2015). Blessingways are a celebration of creation, harmony, and peace. Their original form and purpose were to bless using song, and they were sometimes referred to as the "singing over". These rituals celebrated specific, spiritual rites of passage throughout the entire life cycle, not just the passage into motherhood

(Gordon, 2002; Jones, 2004). Although the mother's blessing retains key aspects of a traditional Blessingways ceremony, it has been westernised and adapted. Most ceremonies are carried out in a circle and include blessings and poems, positive birth stories, empowering words, and songs (Dean, 2020). As a symbolic representation, a birthing necklace may be included, with each guest bringing a bead that means something to them and gifting it to the expectant mother. The beads would be strung together with a beading thread, and each guest would explain the intention or wish behind her choice of bead as she placed it on the string. The finished necklace would then be presented to the mother. During labour, she would wear this necklace, and this would serve as a reminder of all the love, support, and blessings that she had received for her pregnancy and journey into motherhood; a symbolic representation of her belonging to a community of women and mothers (Burns, 2015).

Gordon-Lennox (2017) further elaborates that meaningful ceremonies may include promises, symbolic gestures, and music, coherent with the values of the parents in what they want to transmit to their baby. Moreover, she advises including a pledge from the guide parents, with the baby remaining at the centre of the naming ceremony. Parents choose what kind of elements they think are meaningful, such as music, text, or a physical symbol. The naming ceremony reveals ritualised strategies for giving meaning to birth and this new life, as well as notions of spirituality. The wishes for the baby express a search for meaning and confrontation with the mysterious, as well as moral obligations.

Stories can nurture the capacity for imaginative identifications, and in terms of childbirth, this is the beginning of a story; there are no guarantees, and the story is yet to be revealed, only drawing on the imagined outcome. These stories are found in rituals and ceremonies, with the core values of empathy, compassion, and a sense of justice at the heart.

Naming ceremonies

During the first year of being a parent to twins, I wanted to celebrate their presence in this life, and talking to family members and parents, the custom was for a baptism. With my girlfriends and close relatives, we instead had a naming ceremony, which was intimate and informal. We talked together and made promises to the infants. We welcomed them into the world and celebrated. There was kindness and unity in the ceremony. We also made wooden artefacts for the children to keep – a heart plaque and wooden picture frames. Interestingly, those chosen as guide parents have remained committed to their role. Within the naming ceremony, the key areas I reflected on were empathy, compassion, reason, and respect (Wyman, 1971). This was shared with the babies as the way I want to live.

- Reason: In organising the ceremony, we used the capacity to work things out together. We used reason when forming judgements logically and considered each other.
- Empathy: Having imagined myself in my friends' position being asked to be a godparent when they were not religious, a guide parent made more sense to me and them. I needed to ask how I would feel if we were in their situation.

- Compassion: This was one of the areas we share during the ritual in our promises and how we hope to help the growing children desire to help others who are suffering.

This underpinned my desire to seek out like-minded women in alternative groups, and after the experience of the naming ceremony, I attended mother circles on a more regular basis, with other women who had infants of a similar age.

A women's circle is a safe place for women to gather with intention. In these spaces, their true selves are revealed, and women get to show up as their fully expressed selves. Circles often, as already highlighted, include rituals to mark rites of passages, or to honour the changing seasons and cycles of life. There is usually a theme, and women are invited to share stories and wisdom around the topic. Others listen deeply and don't offer advice or responses. All feelings and expressions are welcome in the circle as a space away from everyday life where emotions can be shared and connections made.

- Circles are a place to reclaim our power, our stories, and our wisdom.
- They allow women to talk without the need to be fixed.
- Circles create opportunities for personal growth.
- They provide places of genuine connection, weaving threads of friendship and support.
- Circles are oxytocin-fuelled fun.

A history of women's circles

Before the rise of patriarchy, religion and community were matriarchal. After all, women create life, and their innate abilities revolved around keeping the tribe alive and nurtured.

Evidence shows communal circle gatherings have long been in existence, and honouring of the divine feminine has long been documented. Circles organised for ritual, storytelling, dance, and singing were commonplace. Today, many indigenous groups still live communally and gather in circles as a part of their culture. These cultures still value the potent healing and enriched communication these gatherings bring.

This collaborative, versatile way of communing and communicating in a non-hierarchical way fosters equality, respect, and connection. Circles can be used to:

- Share individual stories around a chosen theme;
- Celebrate in shared rituals;
- Discuss important topics and share important information;
- Learn new skills or ideas;
- Carry out ceremonies;
- Honour the cycles of the earth like the moon phases;
- Prepare food and meals;
- Sing and dance in community;
- Discuss community needs; and
- Work through and resolve conflicts (King, 1989).

The basic structure of circle gatherings allows everyone's voice to be honoured.

My experience of a mother circle

The group came together and sat around a circular mat and formed a circle. Objects were placed on top of the mat and the circle was therefore created. The objects represented symbols

Figure 7 Circles of care

and alongside the symbols was a long wooden stick, known as a talking stick.

We introduced ourselves one by one and then the use of the stick was explained. When a person holds the stick, they talk about themselves, and the intention is to reflect on feelings connected with them personally about the week or perhaps more broadly. The contributions are not intended to build on previous comments made or extend references associated with the last person to speak. The stick is therefore given to each person to voice their own thoughts and feelings.

Once everybody has spoken, themes are brought together and more openly discussed as a group, and this tends to naturally occur as a result of each person sharing their own experiences. The facilitator of the circle invited each of us to speak. During the time that we spoke, we did not stop and were not interrupted with questions or clarifications about anything by the facilitator. It was just a free space for us to open up the dialogue.

The first mother used her time to speak about her position in her family and their connections. The stick was then handed to a second person who reflected on their feelings of being a new mother and the expectations placed on her in her transitional role. I was then given the stick and invited to talk, and I spoke about the positives and challenges of my week. I shared how this resonated more deeply as a mother in the long term as well as the short term. I felt I was emotionally held in the circle and that I had made connections with each of the other members of the group. It felt like a community, and everybody felt authentically like they were listening to each other. I also felt relaxed and that I could share any aspect of myself. I felt I didn't want to dominate the time by talking too much, and after sharing something, I passed the talking stick back to the facilitator.

At the end of the sharing experiences, one of the mothers asked for the stick again, and she expanded on her initial thoughts about being a new parent. This was then extended further and created an opportunity for everyone to share thoughts and associated feelings, as well as their positions in the community. We discussed how this could be contradictory with our personal feelings about responsibility and being risk-averse as a parent. As a circle, the women were connected and provided a sense of nurturing and belonging. As we spoke together, there was almost an invisible thread connecting each of us as we shared. From the circle, I then shared some ideas about infant massage, which extended the circle discussion. The facilitator then closed the circle and thanked everyone for attending. We had each been able to discuss a positive aspect of ourselves. I initially thought this would be challenging, but when I was given the space to speak, it actually came quite naturally, and I was able to share a positive feeling and an action I had achieved. The circle then closed in a very natural and organic way, and we said our goodbyes and hugged each other as we left the space (www. motherforlife.co.uk/circle-training.php?page=mother-circle-guide-programme).

Organising a circle

In creating a circle, I thought it would be helpful to further consider the elements involved in organising one as part of a community group and how it can be beneficial to new mothers.

When the circle is first organised, there is the intention of creating the circle setting as well as the general intention of the group. The intention is to commune and determine the goals of the gathering. The setting should be convenient for all participants, and spacious enough to physically accommodate everyone comfortably. This can be anything from a hall to a yurt, although room temperature for the infants may be a factor for the success of the group. An overarching theme is selected for the group or specific goals discussed in relation to community engagement, betterment, or conflict resolution. In organising the space, some find it helpful to cleanse it with sage or incense, and light candles. It may also be helpful to prepare the circle's centre with an "altar" highlighting things of meaning related to the circle's theme, where the participants are also welcome to leave a token of their intentions. This space can hold photos or statues of symbols, divination cards, talismans, books, feathers, shells, or sacred water. Items representing the four elements, crystals, or personal artefacts may also be included, but it is the circle members that decide. Fresh or dried flowers, plants, or herbs could also be used. Some groups choose to change the centre each meeting based on their own feelings; some choose to keep it consistent. Some prefer a simple centre like a single candle. Each member is welcomed during the circle to set a positive tone for the gathering.

During the circle:

- Welcome everybody and thank them for attending;
- Open the circle (hold hands, short meditation, read a poem, or other activity);
- Check in… Allow each woman to speak her name and answer a simple question;
- Share your circle guidelines;
- Introduce the theme or gathering;
- Check out… Again each voice is heard; and
- Close circle.

In every circle, under the Gather the Women guidelines, each participant should be responsible for holding the circle. But it is also helpful to have someone in the role of facilitator, and this can be rotated among participants. The facilitator keeps the circle flowing, initiating the opening of the circle, sharing the agreed intention or themes, and starting the check-in process. There may also be a guardian's role, and this is to monitor the mood of the circle and conversation, and call for moments of silence when needed.

Some women find a formal opening, such as casting a circle, calling on the four directions, singing a song or mantra, or sharing a "prayer", is a deeper way to initiate the gathering. They may choose to hold hands and do a group meditation, read a poem based on the theme, do a shared movement, like a dance or yoga stretch, or even do breathing exercises. Some groups may choose to pass out individual instruments for each participant, even as simple as small drums or bells, to participate as a group in making music together. This ritual, whatever is chosen, will help unite and connect the group in a shared ritual experience to establish the connection of the group.

A fundamental rule of being in a circle is for every voice to be heard. This is to dissolve any hierarchy and establish equality among the group. Checking in should begin simply, sharing each participant's name and perhaps answering a common question or speaking on a shared prompt related to the theme. After the check-in, it's important to review the circle's guidelines and intention or reason for coming together. The talking piece is an important element in any circle. This piece can be a stick, as previously discussed, or another item, a sacred object or a simple everyday item like a feather or crystal, that is passed around as people share. The talking piece identifies that the person holding it is the current speaker, and everyone else should be actively listening, and not just waiting to respond. It can be used in two ways, it can be passed clockwise or counterclockwise in order, or it can be placed in the centre and whomever feels called to speak can pick it up to speak and replace it once they are done. The way it is used can shift the flow of conversation and is personal to the group. It is important to note that if anyone chooses not to speak, they are welcome to do so, and after passing on the talking piece in the circle, they may be offered it again in case they have found something to share since they passed on their previous turn. After this, some circles choose to break out into smaller circles to allow for deeper sharing, followed by coming back together to check out. Some may choose to have the whole circle delve deeper into the session's themes, and I think this would depend on both topics and numbers within the group. Others may choose instead to share a group song or dance together in ceremony. Some groups find it helpful to have a set time for the circle meeting as a whole or individual sharing times to keep the sharing flowing. Every group can define their own set of guidelines unique to their goals and intentions. After the circle sharing ends, it's important for everyone's voice to be heard again. This is an opportunity to share and reflect. Closing the circle in a ceremonious way shifts the circle from sacred sharing to a more social time. This can be as simple as thanking everyone for sharing or sharing a chant or meditation. As an inclusive and creative experience, a circle can be customised to a group's particular needs and preferences, but the emphasis is on coming together to share, heal, and grow together, with a unified voice and practice, where everyone is heard and honoured, and with no hierarchy.

Learning objective
Alternative groups as spiritual and social community groups

To begin to understand alternative groups as spiritual and social community groups as a way of bridging personal identity and social identity within groups. To begin to understand the impact of how groups are sought out by women and their needs living within a community.

End note

What is my position as author and researcher in this book?

The main purpose of this book has been to give the reader knowledge and understanding regarding community groups for mothers. The initial chapters were dedicated to thinking about reflection and then this was prompted throughout the subsequent chapters. In each chapter, I wanted to retain mothers' voices, and these have been drawn from my own subjective experiences, as well as anecdotes passed down to me as I became a parent and continued as a professional working with parents. As a psychologist and educator embedded in research and practice, I have always been interested in the differing perspectives on community groups and the purposes they serve for mothers.

The specific areas that I have focused on therefore were the complexities of a caring approach within a community of practice and the lived experiences of mothers with their infants. This was important to me when the area of infant care has often been viewed as passive or less active. I hope therefore that the book has continued to raise awareness about the value of community care and give confidence and trust about how groups can be perceived, fostered, and supported through the relationships formed, as well as enhancing international and tuned in care for infants.

Figure 8 Infant play and care in the community

Observing the interaction between an infant and carer has often been referred to as a dance, with the parent and the infant sharing a moment and responding to each other verbally and non-verbally. They respond to each other and take it in tuns to initiate the conversation and mutually engage. The proto conversation Trevarthen (1993) refers to is a dialogue that does not always include words but reflects to the infant, shows respect, and is in tune with the infant. This includes knowing when the infant is seeking responses and when they have had enough and need to settle within themselves rather than being overwhelmed by the interaction. Discussing community groups provides a rich insight into the way the dancing dialogue can be developed and nurtured between the mother and their infant.

I therefore offer a model of practice of being:

- authentic
- empathetic
- respectful and understanding

while considering aspects of practice within the chapters and including:

- taking the lead from the infant; and
- maintaining respectful relationships with families.

In contextualising mothers' groups, an initial broad perspective about how the groups have been shaped in the past was considered, and examples were included to highlight the complexities of this. Initially, the chapters began with a historical glimpse into the twentieth century and the beginning of hearing women's voices outside mainstream discourses. This was illustrated with the lived experiences in the case studies shared. Revealing and sharing these lived experiences emphasises the power of the collective voice in creating national and political change, with mother and baby homes and the Women's Guild being examples considered.

In exploring groups and what it means to belong and create communities that care during the first year of having an infant, theoretical concepts and conceptual understanding about the power of groups were discussed and evaluated. This focus was intended to provide lived experiences from historical contributions to how mothers were impacted in more recent years by the pandemic. By returning to a new normal and with a national shift in funding, groups offered to mothers to enhance a sense of belonging and connectivity were then explored, and I have included a selected few as illustrations that I consider the reader could align to more examples and thinking about further groups held in the community. I have also threaded through the importance of creating opportunities to reduce stress and support mental health in both the parent and the infant in the earliest years of life.

As a facilitator with some of the groups, I have reflected on what it means to be a mother, as well as the members' narratives shared in the group about what it means to them as they attend. I have consciously attempted to remain inclusive and also include alternative practices, with a focus on their spiritual meanings. Women's circles within and beyond the western view of religious practices have culminated in many women seeking and offering mother's blessings and naming ceremonies rather than baptisms. I therefore reflected on experiences where the community of connection and individual choice was part of the ceremony.

The intention has therefore been to consider the meaning of groups and how they could be beneficial and reach a wide range of community members, fathers included! I hope by exploring these different groups, the book has provided insight and food for thought to widen knowledge and further explore how community groups can be instrumental as a positive and active model in developing and promoting high quality and enriching mother-infant relationships.

Recommended discussion topics

Inclusive groups and questions for discussion

- How could you create an inclusive group?
- If a group has a specific objective and is offering a specialist service, how do you ensure it remains inclusive?
- How could you seek out what new parents living in a local community would benefit from?
- How might you find out what is already successfully being delivered for new parents and mothers in local communities?

Facilitating groups

- Why are community groups for new parents important?
- Why does a sense of belonging and connection make a difference to the lives of new mothers?
- What forms of groups could be established to support new parents?
- How would communities of practice be a central feature in supporting mother-infant relationships?

Project focus

Research groups for new parents.

What types of groups have been successful in the past and why?

- Sing and baby sign groups;
- Baby sensory groups;
- Wriggle and rhyme groups;
- Mother and baby groups; and
- Baby massage groups.

Consider how the groups are:

- financed
- managed
- supported
- facilitated
- resourced
- attended – numbers
- organised – block sessions or one session.

Consider the implications of the above and how groups could remain inclusive irrespective of these factors.

Case study

Paula and her one-year-old triplets have been attending a family centre, initially referred by her local health visitor. She has recently had a knee replacement and has restricted mobility. Her husband is a delivery driver and away during the day and some evenings. They live in a two-bedroom apartment. Paula is beginning to struggle with the triplets as they are becoming increasingly mobile. Her mental health is fragile, and she is increasingly lacking in confidence and avoiding going out. This is exacerbated by the pain in her knee.

How would a community group help? What type of group support might help? What other support might be needed?

What groups have been highlighted in the book that may help Paula?

References

All4Maternity. (2023). *Maternal Journal – Creative Journaling*. [Online] Available at: www.all4maternity.com/maternal-journal-creative-journaling/ [Accessed 21 December 2023].

Bannister, D. (1977). *New Perspectives in Personal Construct Theory*. London: Academic Press.

Bion, R. (1962). *Learning from Experience*. London: Heinemann.

Blair, M. and Macaulay, C. (2014). The Healthy Child Programme: How Did We Get Here and Where Should We Go? *Paediatrics and Child Health*, 24(3), pp. 118–123.

Bloom, K. (1995). The Development of Attachment Behaviours in Pregnant Adolescents. *Nursing Research*, 44(5), pp. 284–289.

Burns, E. (2015). The Blessingway Ceremony: Ritual, Nostalgic Imagination and Feminist Spirituality. *Journal of Religion and Health*, 54(2), pp. 783–797.

Capdevila, R. and Frith, H. (2022). *A Feminist Companion to Research Methods in Psychology: Changing the System not the Person*. London: Oxford University Press.

Choi, P., Henshaw, C., Baker, S. and Tree, J. (2005). Supermum, Superwife, Supereverything: Performing Femininity in the Transition to Motherhood. *Journal of Reproductive and Infant Psychology*, 23(2), pp. 167–180. [Online] Available at: https://doi.org/10.1080/02646830500129487 [Accessed 21 December 2023].

Clough, P. and Corbett, J. (2001). *Theories of Inclusive Practice*. London: Sage.

Cohen, R. (2020). *Margaret Llewelyn Davies: With Women for a New World*. London: Merlin Press.

Dallos, R. (2015). *An Introduction To Family Therapy: Systemic Theory and Practice*. Milton Keynes: Oxford University Press.

Davies, M. L. (1978). *Maternity: Letters from Working Women, Collected by the Women's Co-operative Guild*. London: Virago.

Davies, M. (2014). *Boundary and Space: An Introduction to the Work of D. W. Winnicott*. London: Routledge. DOI: 10.4324/9781315831299.

Dean, D. (2020). Woman's Circles. Available at: www.danielladean.co.uk/woman-circles. [Accessed 31 December 2023].

Dennis, C. and Chung-Lee, L. (2006). Postpartum Depression Help-Seeking Barriers and Maternal Treatment Preferences: A Qualitative Systematic Review. *Birth*, 33(4), pp. 323–331. [Online] Available at: https://doi.org/10.1111/j.1523-536X.2006.00130.x [Accessed 21 December 2023].

Field, T. (2014). Massage Therapy Research Review. *Complementary Therapies in Clinical Practice*, 20, pp. 224–229.

Freud, A. (1966). A Short History of Child Analysis. *Psychoanalytic Study of the Child*, 21, pp. 7–14.

Garvey, C. (2009). *Play* (Enlarged ed.). Cambridge, MA: Harvard University Press.

Gerhardt, S. (2004). *Why Love Matters: How Affection Shapes a Baby's Brain*. London: Routledge.

Godfrey-Issacs, L. (2023) Maternal Journal – Creative Journaling. Available at: www.all4maternity.com [Accessed 1 December 2023].

Gopnik, A. (2016). *The Gardener and the Carpenter: What the New Science of Child Development Tells Us about the Relationship Between Parents and Children*. London: Vintage.

Gordon, C. (2002). Women's Stories: Spiritual Journeys to Herself. *Dissertation Abstracts: Humanities and Social Sciences*. International Section A. 62.

Gordon-Lennox, J. (2017). *Crafting Secular Ritual: A Practical Guide.* London: Jessica Kingsley Publishers.

Hahn, J., Lengerich, A., Byrd, R., Stoltz, R., Hench, J., Byrd, S. and Ford, C. (2016). Neonatal Abstinence Syndrome: The Experience of Infant Massage. *Creative Nursing*, 22(1), pp. 45–50.

Hall, E. (2021) *Born in Lockdown*. [Online]. Available at: www.mothershipwriters.com/borninlockdown.   [Accessed   31 December 2023]. Hayward, R. (2009) Enduring Emotions: James L. Halliday and the Invention of the Psychosocial. *Isis Journal*, 100(4), pp. 827–838.

hooks, b. (1984). *Feminist Theory: From Margin to Centre.* London: South End Press.

hooks, b. (1999). *All About Love.* New York: William and Morrow PB.

Jones, J. (2004). Mother Blessings, Cultural Appropriation and What to Do Instead. Newborn Mothers. [Online] Available at: https://newbornmothers.com/blog/mother-blessings-cultural-appropriation-and-what-to-do-instead [Accessed 12 December 2020].

Kelly, G. (1955, 2013). *A Theory of Personality: The Psychology of Personal Constructs.* London: Norton.

King, V. (1993). *Women and Spirituality.* London: MacMillan.

Klaus, M., Kennell, J. and Klaus, P. (1995*). Bonding: Building the Foundation of a Secure Attachment and Independence.* Reading, MA: Addison-Wesley.

Leach, P. (Ed.). (2017). *Transforming Infant Wellbeing: Research, Policy and Practice for the First 1001 Critical Days.* London: Routledge.

Leavy, P. and Harris, X. (2018). *Contemporary Feminist Research from Theory to Practice.* Guildford: Guilford Publications.

Matthews, S. H. (2005). Crafting Qualitative Research Articles on Marriages and Families. *Journal of Marriage and Family*, 67, pp. 799–808.

Mcleod, S. (2023). Social Identity Theory. In: *Psychology*. Available at: www.simplypsychology.org/social-identity-theory.html.

Mellow Parenting (2023). *An Overview of the Project Mellow Parenting.* [Online] Available at: www.mellowparenting.org/ [Accessed 21 December 2023].

Montagu, A. (1986). *Touching: The Human Significance of the Skin.* 3rd ed. New York: Harper Row Publishers, Inc.

Mother for Life (2023) *An Introduction.* [Online] Available at: www.motherforlife.co.uk/circle-training.php?page=mother-circle-guide-programme [Accessed 21 December 2023].

Mothers for Mothers (2023). *Our Impact.* [Online] Available at: https://mothersformothers.co.uk/our-impact-2022-2023/ [Accessed 21 December 2023].

Mothership Writers (2023) *Born in Lockdown.* [Online] Available at: www.mothershipwriters.com/borninlockdown [Accessed 21 December 2023].

Movement for an Adoption Apology. (2023). *Stories – Birth Mothers.* [Online] Available at: https://movementforanadoptionapology.org/your-stories/#:~:text=I%20became%20pregnant%20at%20age,friends%20realised%20and%20told%20her [Accessed 21 December 2023].

Norman, A. (2022). *Historical Perspectives on Infant Care.* London: Bloomsbury.

Odent, M. (2001). New Reasons and New Ways to Study Birth Physiology. *International Journal of Gynecology & Obstetrics*, 75, pp. S39–S45.

Porter, L. S., Porter, B. O., McCoy, V., Bango-Sanchez, V., Kissel, B., Williams, M. and Nunnewar, S. (2015). Blended Infant Massage-Parenting Enhancement Program on Recovering Substance-Abusing Mothers' Parenting Stress, Self Esteem, Depression, Maternal Attachment, and Mother-Infant Interaction. *Asian Nursing Research*, 9, pp. 318–327.

Pownal, M. (2021). *A Feminist Companion to Social Psychology*. London: Oxford University Press.

Rockabye (2023). *Testimonials*. [Online] Available at:www.rocka bye.org.uk/testimonials/ [Accessed 21 December 2023].

Rogers, C. R. (1980). *A Way of Being*. Houghton Mifflin Harcourt.

Seifert, K. and Mandzuk, D. (2006). Student Cohorts in Teacher Education: Support Groups or Intellectual Communities? *Teachers College Record*, 108(7), pp. 1296–1320.

Seppälä, T., Riikonen, R., Paajanen, P., Stevenson, C. and Finell, E. (2022). Development of First-Time Mothers' Sense of Shared Identity and Integration with Other Mothers in Their Neighbourhood. *Journal of Community & Applied Social Psychology*, 32(4), pp. 692–705. [Online] Available at: https://doi. org/10.1002/casp.2592 [Accessed 21 December 2023].

Sturme, A. (2015). A Time to Heal: Mother Blessing. [Online] Available at: www.danielladean.co.uk/woman-circles [Accessed 31 December 2023].

Tajfel, H. (1979). Individuals and Groups in Social Psychology. *British Journal of Social and Clinical Psychology*, 18(2), pp. 183–190.

Tajfel, H., Turner, J. C., Austin, W. G., and Worchel, S. (1979). An Integrative Theory of Intergroup Conflict. In: M. A. Hogg and D. Abrams, eds., *Organizational Identity: A Reader*. London: Psychology Press, pp. 56–65.

Thane, P. (2011). Unmarried Motherhood in Twentieth-Century England. *Women's History Review*, 20(1), pp. 11–29.

Thomas, A. and Chess, S. (1977). *Temperament and Development*. Oxford: Brunner/Mazel.

Tilghman, C. (2003). Autobiography as Dissidence: Subjectivity, Sexuality, and the Women's Co-operative Guild. *Biography*, 26(4), pp. 583–606. Available at: http://www.jstor.org/stable/23540443 [Accessed 21 December 2023].

Trevarthen, C. (1993). Predispositions to Cultural Learning in Young Infants. *Behavioral and Brain Sciences*, 16(3), pp. 534–535.

Twins Trust (2023). *Home Page*. [Online] Available at: www.twinstr ust.org. [Accessed 21 December 2023].

Wenger, E. (1998). *Communities of Practice: Learning, Meaning and Identity*. Cambridge: Cambridge University Press.

Winnicott, D. (1953). Transitional Objects and Transitional Phenomena – a Study of the First Not-Me Possession. *International Journal of Psycho-Analysis*, 34, pp. 89–97.

Winnicott, D. (1968). *Family and Individual Development*. London: Routledge.

Wyman, L. C. (1971) Blessingway. *American Anthropologist*, 73(6), pp. 1360–1361. [Online] Available at: https://anthrosource. onlinelibrary.wiley.com/doi/pdf/10.1525/aa.1971.73.6.02a00520 [Accessed 21 December 2023].

Recommended further reading

Geldard, K. (2001). *Working with Children in Groups: A Handbook for Counsellors, Educators and Community Workers*. London: Palgrave.

Grimmer, T. (2021). *Developing a Loving Pedagogy in the Early Years: How Love Fits with Professional Practice*. London: Routledge

Hooks, B. (2003). *The Will to Change: Men, Masculinity, and Love*. New York: Atria Books.

Hooks, B. (2008). *Belonging*. London: Routledge.

Lave, J. and Wenger, E. (1991). *Situated Learning: Legitimate Peripheral Participation*. Cambridge: Cambridge University Press.

Simpson, R. (2001). Baby Massage Classes and the Work of the International Association of Infant Massage. *Complementary Therapies in Nursing and Midwifery*, 7(1), pp. 25–33. [Online] Available at: https://doi.org/10.1054/ctnm.2000.0510 [Accessed 21 December 2023].

Index